KAREN WINTER

Romance Tropes: Enemies to Lovers

A reference tool for plotting romance stories – covering all romance genres

First published by Fountain Pen Publishing Limited 2020

First edition

ISBN: 978-0-473-52042-7

Editing by Lesley Marshall

This book was professionally typeset on Reedsy.
Find out more at reedsy.com

Contents

Dedication

For Animals

"The question is, are we happy to suppose that our grandchildren may never be able to see an elephant except in a picture book?"

Sir David Attenborough

Introduction

What if ... you return to your hometown intending to take over and run the family B&B, but you find out it's in financial trouble and the man you've never been able to forget is working for a company that intends to buy it? Or maybe your boyfriend left town after you were in a car accident and now he's back.

Or, what if ... your drug addict mother comes home one night with a purse full of cash, so you run off with your sister and the purse hoping to start a new life, but when you move into an apartment the guy next door's a detective and intent on getting to know you? Or you settle down with your adopted daughter in a quiet country town, but her biological father arrives on your doorstep, intending to take his daughter home with him?

Enemies to Lovers—he may be the sexiest man alive but that doesn't mean you forgive him his sins, or that you can even tolerate being in the same room without him ruffling your feathers!

What is the appeal of the enemies-to-lovers trope and why do readers keep coming back for more?

Perhaps it's witnessing the characters going through an internal struggle as they battle between their annoyance or even hatred towards the other, but still find there's physical attraction. And then they discover the other's endearing side that's in outright conflict with their indignant right to be angry with them.

As the name suggests, the enemies-to-lovers trope has an inevitable plot scenario whereby the characters start off their story at a point then they're in some way miffed or angry with each other, but as the story progresses this couple sort out their differences and fall in love. The two may have past history, or they may only just have met, but are immediately thrown into a difficult situation with inevitable conflict between them. Either way, this tension and conflict between them during their journey is what the reader is looking for.

So how do we create unique stories that feature a couple who start off as enemies but end up as lovers?

By researching the stories that have already been published and looking for ways to add an original plot twist or combine plot points from several stories to create an exciting journey for your characters.

This book has been written to provide you, the romance writer, with an extensive resource of story examples written in this trope. By the time you've finished reading the book you will have a wealth of knowledge to assist you in coming up with new and different plot scenarios for your own stories.

Definition of Enemies to Lovers

The following is the definition of "enemies to lovers" I used in my book **Romance Tropes and Hooks**:

The hero and heroine start out as enemies, e.g. business rivals, family feud, law enforcement and criminal, etc. or hating each other over some past event. They are on opposing sides and neither will concede or compromise, until their quarrelling turns to romance and they eventually fall in love.

Note: The "enemies to lovers" trope has an "enemies" scale ranging from slightly miffed with each other through to I totally hate you, or I'm going to bring you down.

General Guidelines for Writing this Trope

The enemies-to-lovers trope can be the primary trope for a story, or it can be used in conjunction with several other tropes.

This trope is basically centred on the conflict between the hero and heroine while they work out their differences or resolve the situation that has caused them to become enemies—but the conflict must happen organically as an outcome of their past and present actions, or those of someone else.

Typically the story will start with the reader finding out what caused these two characters to be in conflict, and this conflict can have a wide range of annoyance/adversary levels, from a personality clash through to blackmail or revenge, and may include being on opposite sides of the law.

So with this wide scale available for you to come up with your "enemies" starting point, you can base your story plot on pretty much any situation where your characters are in conflict. For example:

- They have a difference of opinion or personality clash,

- They are business rivals, or competing against each other,
- They are involved in a business takeover,
- One has captured or kidnapped the other,
- One is blackmailing the other,
- They are on opposite sides of the law,
- They are simply on opposite sides of a dispute, or have opposing goals,
- They have a marriage of convenience where one or both characters feel forced into it,
- One feels unfairly treated by the other,
- Someone else is interfering in their life, which is causing friction between them,
- One character is resentful or out for revenge because of a deed done by the other,
- They are from opposing sides of a family or business feud,
- They are both investigating a crime, but from different standpoints,
- They are in conflict over what's best for someone else – a child, or other family member.

Once you've come up with an "enemies" situation and are starting to work on the plot scenario, try to come up with something unique or slightly quirky so that your story has a point of difference to others in the same plot scenario category.

Your reader needs to see your characters' personalities and circumstances at the beginning of your story so they can then see their personal growth by the end. If your ending is going to work for your reader, they need to have been watching your characters change over the course of the book while they're working through the conflict caused by the "enemies" situation, so the now different stance of both characters is entirely believable.

What character wounds could you give your protagonists that will become aggravated as a result of the other character's behaviour or lack of understanding or empathy towards the situation?

What flaws do your characters possess as a result of this wound? What does the other character do to antagonise and inflame their feelings? Do they become enraged by the injustice of the situation or is their personality more slanted towards quiet, self-pitying reflection?

Make sure you establish your character's motivation—what they fear or desire—so the reader has something to root for or to dread on their behalf. Your reader will want to immerse herself in the story and participate in it through your characters—particularly the heroine—so make sure you employ visceral responses and high emotions as she mentally processes the situation. What choices does she have and what are the possible consequences of those choices? And what reasons does she have for making her decisions?

Create a strong bond between your reader and the heroine because your reader will be experiencing the story vicariously through the heroine. So when she feels indignant and distressed by the hero's words or actions you want your reader to feel the same burn and tightness inside. Your reader needs to be cheering for your characters and feel empathy for their circumstances.

Typically, the main part of the story will focus on the characters getting on with their life and working out how to deal with each other and come to terms with the situation. This is where they get to know each other better, or see the other in a different light—perhaps understanding the other person's circumstances more and feeling less aggrieved and more open to compromise, or even dropping altogether the issue that caused the confrontation in the first place. This is where we see our characters grow and where mutual respect is formed.

The last part of the story will wind up the issues and focus on the couple contemplating their future. This may include the characters admitting their feelings for each other despite what has happened. They must sort out their disagreements so they can have their happy ever after.

For the reader, the enjoyment of this romance trope is the slow burn of the couple initially hating each other, developing mutual respect and then slowly becoming lovers—and falling in love.

Publishers are always keen to be offered manuscripts that feature a fresh twist on this classic romance trope, so add your own personality to make it uniquely yours. Look for fresh ways to rejuvenate this classic trope. For instance, instead of going for the simple "enemies to lover" situation, why not make it "friends to enemies to lovers", or "unrequited love to enemies to lovers", or "co-workers to enemies to lovers"?

The Stories

The following pages contain a collection of stories where "enemies to lovers" is one of the tropes used—either as the primary story trope or as a secondary trope that enhances the main plot.

For your reference I've included the story description from Amazon's book pages at the time of writing this book—the genre and main tropes used are also noted.

They are in alphabetical order so you can find a story you want to refer back to when you're using the categorised lists I've included at the end. You can also find a story through the index at the front of this book.

Please note:

1. *For some stories there wasn't enough information in the book description to work out how the enemies-to-lovers scenario was incorporated. In these situations I used the customer reviews to get a more complete understanding of the plot—hence there may be additional details in the enemies-to-lovers scenario explanation that aren't in the*

book description.

2. *For the plot scenarios I focussed on the situation that caused the hero and heroine to become "enemies".*

3. *There were a lot of stories where this trope was used. Therefore, I have tried to include a variety of story scenarios—not just those with classic enemies-to-lovers plots, but ones that had a twist on this classic plot. I also looked for stories where I thought the plot could be expanded on or used in a different context. Some plot scenarios featured in many books, so I chose just a few examples or picked ones that had a more comprehensive plot outline.*

69 Million Things I Hate About You

By Kira Archer

After personal assistant Kiersten Abbott wins sixty-nine million dollars in the lotto, she suddenly has more than enough money to quit her impossibly demanding job. But where's the fun in that? She decides to stay and exact a little revenge on her insufferable ass of a boss.

Billionaire Cole Harrington quickly figures out something's afoot with his usually agreeable personal assistant. When he finds out about the office pool betting on how long it'll take him to fire her, he decides to spice things up and see how far he can push her until she quits.

The game is on, with everyone waiting to see who will crack first. But the bet sparks a new dynamic between them, and soon they realize they just might have crossed that fine line between hate and love.

Tropes: Enemies to Lovers, Bet/Dare/Wager, Boss and Employee, Opposites Attract, Revenge

Genre: Contemporary

Enemies to Lovers Scenario – Heroine feels unfairly treated by the hero

The heroine is the hero's personal assistant and she feels he places ridiculous demands on her, expecting her to be available 24/7 for whatever whim he demands. When she and her friends win the lottery, instead of quitting her job she decides to exact a little satisfying revenge by deliberately being terrible at her job. When the hero finds out there's an office pool on how long it will take him to fire her he decides to join the fun. But as sparks fly between them their irritation with each other crosses the line into something quite different.

A Lady Never Tells

By Lynn Winchester

Richard Downing may be a viscount of impeccable character, but he's bored beyond belief of dancing at balls, faking smiles, and making dull conversation. So when he stumbles upon a housemaid with defiance in her striking blue eyes and a dagger hidden in her skirts...well, color him intrigued.

Raised with a rather...peculiar upbringing, Lady Victoria Daring is full of secrets and surprises. As part of His Majesty's personal homeland spy network and as a master of disguises, Vic is charged with infiltrating high society to uncover the enemies hiding in plain sight.

But Richard is the first man to see through her disguises––and infiltrate deep into her heart. Too bad his family is at the top of her list of suspects...

Tropes: Enemies to Lovers, Bodyguard/Protector

Genre: Historical

Enemies to Lovers Scenario – Opposite sides of the law

The heroine is a spy working for His Majesty's personal homeland network and she's been tasked with infiltrating high society to uncover enemies—with the hero's family being at the top of her list.

A Man of Honor

By Miranda Liasson

He survived combat...but will he fight for love?

Former Army Captain and venture capitalist Preston Guthrie has always had a thing for Cat Kingston, but he never felt like he could date his best friend's sister. Plus, he's a wrong-side-of-the-tracks guy and she's a white-picket-fence kind of woman. Yet when they met again just before he was deployed, sparks flew. A fire ignited. And the heat was hot. For the first time, he thought a relationship with her might be possible...until an injury in the war changed everything...

Journalist Cat Kingston had a rough couple of years, surviving a broken engagement and the loss of her job. But connecting with Preston last fall seemed right. They shared steamy Skype sessions while he was overseas—until he was wounded, and cut her off without explanation. Now he's back in town to be the Best Man for her sister's wedding...and she wants answers.

Preston's struggling with a leg wound, but the war scarred him on the inside, too. When Cat pays him a surprise visit and her brother catches them in a compromising position, Preston tells him they're dating. He's not sure how he can spend the entire wedding week fake-dating her when the chemistry between them feels anything but...

Tropes: Enemies to Lovers, Across the Tracks, Bad Boy/Bachelor/Playboy Reformed

Genre: Contemporary

Enemies to Lovers Scenario — Heroine feels unfairly treated by the hero

The hero and heroine kept in contact via Skype while he was overseas fighting in the war, but he breaks contact with her after he gets wounded. When he returns to town to attend a wedding, she wants answers.

A Millionaire at Midnight

By Naima Simone

Boston socialite Morgan Lett is having a run of bad luck. Her fiancé just dumped her for her stepsister, the charity foundation she's given her life to is in danger of folding, and now, the gorgeous man she bid on and won at a masquerade bachelor auction turns out to be a cold-hearted jerk...and her new employer.

Millionaire Alexander Bishop needs the best wife money can buy. In order to inherit his family business, he must get engaged—fast. And Morgan, with her beauty and pedigree, is the perfect candidate. Her sharp tongue may drive him crazy, but she needs money to save the foundation she loves, and he needs a fiancée. It's a flawless arrangement—no strings, no love. But soon she has him craving more, and cursing the platonic terms of their agreement.

Still, he won't allow need—no matter how hot it burns—to threaten everything he's built.

Tropes: Enemies to Lovers, Boss and Employee, Fake Engagement

Genre: Contemporary

Enemies to Lovers Scenario – Clash of personalities
The hero overhears the heroine saying that she's on the hunt for a rich man who's good in the sack and thinks she's just another gold digger. Things go from bad to worse when she wins a date with him at a bachelor auction and then he discovers she's the executive assistant at the company he's just acquired. Later, in exchange for him giving her the money she needs to help save a charity close to her heart, she agrees to a fake engagement with him because he needs a fiancée to cement a position with his family company.

A Mistress for Penndrake

By Tammy L. Bailey

The Marquess of Wesley is out for blood. For a year, Lord Wesley has tried to undo the devastation his father left to Penndrake, their ancestral home, only to discover the man gambled it away right before his death. Now Wesley is being blackmailed by the new owner into marrying a woman he's never met in order to get it back. But his intentions are less than honorable...

At one and twenty, Miss Kate Holden intends to become a governess, having sworn off all men years ago. However, her plans are halted when she receives a daunting letter from her cousin about a Lord Wesley. Ignorant of the name, and the devilish marquess that wears it all too well, she nearly ends up compromised. Refusing to fall prey to Wesley's skillful seduction, Kate decides to turn things around on the rake. But the high-stakes game between them soon leads to her losing the last thing she expected...her heart.

Tropes: Enemies to Lovers, Arranged Marriage, Blackmail, Revenge

Genre: Historical

Enemies to Lovers Scenario – Interference by others

The hero is being blackmailed into marrying the hero-ine—someone he's never met—in order to get back the ancestral home his father gambled away. Annoyed at being dictated to, he decides to ruin the woman he's being forced to marry, but he soon realises she isn't the sort of woman one can ruin without consideration. The blackmailer has regrets over his actions and warns the heroine about the hero. Not knowing the details regarding the warning, she decides to keep clear of the hero at all costs. But no matter how hard this couple try to dislike each other their mutual attraction can't be suppressed.

A Moment of Madness

By Brooklyn Skye

Chemistry that can make them lose their heads...and their hearts.

Sailor Carlson comes back to Boston to make amends with her dad, only to find he passed away, and his bar, the Alibi, now belongs to a bearded, grumpy hottie. Mr. Hottie liked her enough for a night of nameless sex on the kitchen counter, but he wants nothing to do with her now he knows who she is.

Ryan Edwards has been running the Alibi for seven years. Being in a bar night after night means he's no stranger to one-night stands. But when the quirky, beautiful blonde he spent a hot night with shows up at his bar claiming it used to belong to her father, his guard goes right up.

Ryan's desperate for a waitress, and Sailor wants a chance to work in the place that meant so much to her dad. If only the tenuous trust they establish were as strong as the pesky attraction simmering between them.

Tropes: Enemies to Lovers, One-Night Stand

Genre: Contemporary

Enemies to Lovers Scenario – Resentment
 The heroine returns home to find out her father has passed away and his bar now belongs to the hero. They are both resentful and wary of each other, but the heroine wants the opportunity to work at the place that meant so much to her father and the hero is desperate for a waitress.

A Pirate's Command

By Meg Hennessy

His secrets could destroy her...

New Orleans, 1817

Colette Kincaid once knew such love and delicious passion in the arms of her pirate husband, Donato de la Roche. Yet Colette could not continue to live as the wife of a pirate, when reunited with her family. So she fled, taking their son with her and reconciling herself to never seeing her husband again...

Until their son is taken.

Donato is convinced his wife is behind his son's disappearance—just as she is convinced he is the villain. Now they're unable to leave each other's side as they seek their child, forced to confront the desire that still smolders between them. But Donato knows that soon he must face the secret about Colette he's been hiding for so long. And it's a secret for which there is no forgiveness...

Tropes: Enemies to Lovers, Forced Proximity, Marriage in Trouble, Second Chance

Genre: Historical

Enemies to Lovers Scenario – Resentment

The hero is a pirate and he's married to the heroine, but she can't continue to live as the wife of a pirate so she returns to her family, taking their son with her. When someone kidnaps their child they blame each other—however they'll need to work together to find him.

A Rogue for Emily

By Catherine Hemmerling

Emily Moss cannot stand the roguish Alexander Bredon. As this season's most desired debut, she could have any man she wants. Unfortunately, Lady Lancaster pairs her up with none other than the incorrigible man himself.

With mutual dislike and contempt, Alex would rather be doing anything other than escorting the high and mighty Emily, until a secret about her falls into his lap. Suddenly, he realizes there may be more to the lady than he originally thought.

Perhaps the only thing that can keep them from killing each other is falling for each other instead.

Tropes: Enemies to Lovers

Genre: Historical

Enemies to Lovers Scenario – Clash of personalities
    The hero and heroine have never liked each—she thinks he is sexist towards her, and he finds she never has anything kind

to say to him. But they are paired up for a mission so have no choice but to spend time together.

A Vengeful Affair

By Carmen Falcone

Rich people get away with murder every day, but Vivian Foster intends to make billionaire Javier Rivera pay for what he did to her best friend—and how better to destroy a money-grubbing bastard than to sabotage the merger that means everything to him.

Javier Rivera would never hurt a woman much less kill one. But when he catches a gorgeous corporate spy in his office, he knows he can't let her go—not when even a hint of scandal could ruin his career. Until the merger is signed, he'll keep her close, even if he has to shackle her to his wrist. Literally.

But the closer Javier gets to Vivian, the more he wants her, and the more time she spends with him, the less she believes he could ever be a killer. Now Vivian and Javier have to discover the truth...and Vivian has to win the trust of her worst enemy.

Tropes: Enemies to Lovers, Forced Proximity, Revenge

Genre: Contemporary

Enemies to Lovers Scenario – Resentment

The heroine believes the hero was responsible for the demise of her best friend so she's going to make him pay by sabotaging the merger he's working on.

An Accidental Date with a Billionaire

By Diane Alberts

Samantha Matthews turned her back on her wealthy family to focus on social work. Those who know her think she's the heart of kindness. Those who know her really well know she's in a never-ending battle to make up for the harm her family's companies inflict on the world. Which is how she finds herself at a charity bachelor auction of all places.

But oops, she was supposed to bid on her bff's brother as a favor and accidentally bid on the wrong guy. Sue her for not being able to tell one stick-in-the-mud CEO from another.

Backstage, she goes to tell him not to worry about having to go through with a date or anything, but the oafish billionaire cuts her off dismissively. Looks her up and down, hands her a card with his assistant's contact details, and reminds her that sex is definitely off the table.

Oh, she'll call the assistant all right and have her make sure he wears jeans and comfortable shoes and to pick her up at seven a.m. The only "hammering" this guy is going to be doing is at

Habitat for Humanity.

Too bad he turns out to be nothing like she expected.

Tropes: Enemies to Lovers, Mistaken Identity, Opposites Attract

Genre: Contemporary

Enemies to Lovers Scenario – Clash of personalities

When the heroine accidentally bids on the wrong CEO at a charity auction she's about to call the whole thing off but the hero insults her—so now she's hatching a plan to put him right in his place.

An Artful Seduction

By Tina Gabrielle

1815 London

His lust for revenge will be his downfall...

Eliza Somerton has a dangerous secret. As the daughter of the infamous art forger who duped half the ton, she's rebuilt her life under a new name. But when an old forgery goes up for auction, her father's enemy, Grayson Montgomery, outbids her and presents her with an unimaginable choice: help him find her father or he'll ruin her.

For years, Grayson, the Earl of Huntingdon and one of London's top art critics, has sought justice. His well-laid plans finally come to fruition when he learns of his enemy's beautiful daughter. But Eliza possesses a sensuality and independent spirit that weakens his resolve, and as the heat between them sizzles, what started as revenge soon blossoms into something sinful...

Tropes: Enemies to Lovers, Blackmail, Revenge

Genre: Historical

Enemies to Lovers Scenario – Revenge

The hero is the enemy of the heroine's father, and he seeks justice for the art forger having duped half the ton. He blackmails the heroine into helping him find her father so he can turn the man in—if she refuses he'll ruin her.

Armed 'N' Ready

By Tee O'Fallon

Massachusetts State Police Sgt. Nick Houston is as tough as they come, and he and his K-9, Saxon, are hot on the trail of a major illegal gun dealer. But his best lead—the beautiful owner of the Dog Park Café, Andi Hardt––is not cooperating. Doesn't matter how sexy she is or that his dog seems to be in love with her. She's a suspect, and he won't cross that line. Ever.

Andi Hardt sank everything into her dream business—the Dog Park Café, a restaurant catering to dogs as much as people. Now everything is in jeopardy because of one extremely frustrating, incredibly hot state trooper. Like it or not, she's in Nick's crosshairs, and he's calling the shots. Her only option: cooperate, or lose everything she's worked so hard for.

Nick and Andi are catapulted straight into the danger zone, forcing them to make life-altering choices and face their desires. Risking his life for Andi is the easy part. Risking his heart is the toughest assignment Nick will face.

Tropes: Enemies to Lovers, Bodyguard/Protector, Opposites

Attract

Genre: Romantic Suspense

Enemies to Lovers Scenario – Clash of personalities
The hero is after a major illegal gun dealer and his best lead is the heroine but she's not cooperating. The heroine's business is in jeopardy due to the hero's suspicion that she's involved, so the only way to get him off her back is to cooperate.

Asking for Trouble

By Tessa Bailey

The fighting was just foreplay...

Brent Mason and Hayden Winstead can't stand each other. She plans exclusive parties for her rich family's charities. He's a rough and tumble cop who rigs explosives for a living. Could two people be any less suited for conversation? They think not and prefer to keep it that way.

Unfortunately, their two best friends are deeply, disgustingly in love. Forced together, the mutual attraction simmering beneath the surface of Brent and Hayden's non-relationship grows with every argument until it explodes into a scintillating night of mind-blowing sex. And it won't be the last, as far as Brent's concerned.

Hayden has a secret, though. Her father's company is relying on a merger to save them from financial ruin, and only Hayden's marriage to the CEO's wealthy son can secure the deal. If she's to protect her family, she'll have to forget Brent. And he has no intention of being forgotten.

Tropes: Enemies to Lovers, Forced Proximity, Opposites Attract

Genre: Contemporary

Enemies to Lovers Scenario – Clash of personalities

The hero and heroine have mutual friends which means they often end up being in the same room but that only brings out the worst in them—a dislike for each other is just the starting point, until their explosive arguments end up in a night of mind-blowing sex. But the heroine must marry the son of a wealthy CEO to secure a deal and prevent her father's company from financial ruin; however the hero has other ideas.

At the Spy's Pleasure

By Tina Gabrielle

Every gentleman has his secrets...

London 1821

After years of marriage to a selfish man who preferred gambling to his young bride, Jane, the widowed countess of Stanwell, now seeks what she was long denied—a satisfying lover. Naturally, a lady needs a list of eligible candidates, which doesn't include the dangerously handsome (if far too arrogant) Gareth Ramsey...until he steals a sinful kiss from Jane's all-too-willing lips.

Reputed as an arrogant barrister, Gareth's real occupation is as a spy in the service of His Majesty, and his suspect is on Jane's list of possible lovers. With her life in danger, there's no safer place for Jane than with him-and in his bed. But Jane is as distracting as she is infuriating, and keeping her by his side while he pursues his mission might just endanger them both...

Tropes: Enemies to Lovers, Bodyguard/Protector, Second

Chance

Genre: Historical

Enemies to Lovers Scenario – Clash of personalities
   The heroine is putting together a list of gentlemen she thinks will be suitable as a lover, although she's most definitely not putting the hero's name on her list since he's far too arrogant in her opinion. The hero is masquerading as an arrogant barrister to conceal his real occupation of a spy, and one of his suspects is on the heroine's list—giving him a good reason to keep her in his bed where she'll be safe.

Awakening: Britton

By Abby Niles

"I would lick that man up one side and down the other."

Half-shifter and lead SPAC agent, Val Calhoun has listened to women gush over the Don Juan of the precinct for the last four years. Yeah, Detective Britton Townsend is hot and has stunning blue eyes, but that foul mouth he saves only for her? What a waste of good looks. And no way does Val want that mouth anywhere near hers.

When the shifter community is threatened, Val is assigned to the case...and fails. So the High Council turns to the rogue shifter they'd sentenced to twenty years as a human—that same obnoxiously sexy Detective Townsend. And sends the two arch-enemies deep into the North Carolina Mountains—together, and alone.

Being stuck in a tiny honeymoon cabin with Miss Castration and only one bed is definitely not Britton's idea of a good time. But the High Council doesn't take no for an answer. After his shifter abilities are restored, Brit is once again susceptible to the dreaded, irreversible bonding instinct, the Drall. Thankfully, all he's ever felt for Val is intense loathing, no reason to worry. Right? All he has to do is solve this case pronto, and he can go back to his footloose Casanova ways. That is, if they don't kill each other first. Or worse...fall in love.

Tropes: Enemies to Lovers, Forced Proximity

Genre: Paranormal

Enemies to Lovers Scenario – Resentment

The hero feels resentment towards the heroine because she took his job as head of the SPAC; meanwhile the heroine dislikes the hero's attitude, and his flagrant flirting and bedding of women. Now they have to team up on a high-stakes ransom case which requires them to spend several days together in a cabin in the mountains.

Bad Mouth

By Angela McCallister

After her ex-husband's obsession with vampires, Valerie Craig is on a mission to stop transformations. Of all vampires, Kade Rollins is the worst of the worst, but when multiple murders plague Seattle, Val is forced to enlist his aid. Kade's crude wit and seductive nature attract her like no other, but she can't ignore his violence towards his human servants, no matter her yearning to forget.

She's torn when she learns Kade may be behind the murders. Val's worked hard to protect humans from vampires, but the truth surrounding the murders could ignite a bloody battle between their races, one humans are sure to lose. Someone is pulling strings to build a vampire army and spark the war — setting Kade up to kick it off. But if she trusts the vampire prince, she risks her job, her integrity, and her heart if he betrays her as all the men in her life have.

Tropes: Enemies to Lovers

Genre: Paranormal

Enemies to Lovers Scenario – Clash of personalities

The hero is a cocky vampire who's been tasked with helping the heroine solve a slew of murders. The heroine is well-bred and on the serious side so she's annoyed with the hero's crass language and blunt way of saying things.

Beauty and the Bachelor

By Naima Simone

Billionaire Lucas Oliver is hell-bent on revenge. And his plan begins when Sydney Blake—the stunning daughter of his enemy—is tricked into bidding on Lucas at a bachelor auction. Then he serves up a little blackmail...followed by a marriage proposal Sydney has no choice but to accept.

Sydney has been controlled by her family her whole life. When Lucas threatens to reveal her father's shady business, she is once again forced to do her duty for her family. But worse—oh so much worse—is the rush of lust that Lucas ignites in her blood.

Lucas is determined to get his revenge, but it's tough when he can't keep from touching her—or thinking about touching her—all the time. She's not faring much better since she's engaged to a darkly handsome beast intent on destroying her entire family...along with her heart.

Tropes: Enemies to Lovers, Blackmail, Forced Marriage, Revenge

Genre: Contemporary

Enemies to Lovers Scenario – Revenge

The hero is seeking revenge against the heroine's father and decides to use the heroine as bait. He blackmails her into marriage by threatening to expose her father's shady business dealings.

Beauty and the Werewolf

By Kristin Miller

This lone wolf falls hard...for his enemy.

Unmated werewolves don't normally live past three hundred years old...and billionaire Jack MacGrath is cutting it close. Sure, he has almost everything—the respect of his peers, a mansion in San Francisco, a private jet, and fast cars. But without a mate, Jack's in trouble. Then he sees her. Gorgeous, proud...and his enemy.

Isabelle Connelly is good at hiding things from her father. Like her success as a painter, or the incredibly intense attraction she has to Jack MacGrath. After all, she's royalty and falling for anyone lesser—to say nothing of a rival pack—would be, er, unseemly. Now she must choose between her duty to her family and her pack...or her perfect fated mate.

Tropes: Enemies to Lovers, Across the Tracks, Bad Boy/Bachelor/Playboy Reformed, Forbidden Love/Off Limits, Royalty

Genre: Paranormal

Enemies to Lovers Scenario – Interference by others

The hero is an unmated werewolf who needs a mate to stay alive. When he sees the heroine he wants her because he recognises she's the one—his fated mate—but their packs are enemies. The heroine already struggles with gaining her father's approval, and falling in love with the hero makes that even harder.

Besting the Billionaire

By Alison Aimes

Billionaire Alexander Kazankov always wins. But he didn't count on high-heeled, drop-dead sexy Lily Bennett getting in the way of his latest deal. She's a distraction he doesn't need, not when he's so close to making things right for his family.

Lily may walk and talk like a Southern piece of fluff, but she's been underestimated before. She's determined to succeed—and no entitled, arrogant asshole, especially the too-gorgeous-for-his-own-good-kind, is going to get in her way.

Oil meet water. Gasoline meet spark. It's all-out war as these two enemies go toe-to-toe in an ugly, take no prisoners battle to prove they're the right choice to be CEO of the same company. All too soon playing dirty in the boardroom leads to playing even dirtier in the dark. It's destined to end in personal and professional disaster. So why the hell can't they stop?

Tropes: Enemies to Lovers, Co-workers

Genre: Contemporary

Enemies to Lovers Scenario – Business rivals/Competing against each other

The hero and heroine are competing for the position of CEO of the same company.

Betraying the Billionaire

By Victoria Davies

Julian Worth isn't a man with time to spare. Ruling his billion dollar empire with an iron fist, work is the true love of his life. Which is why when it comes to marriage, a strategic alliance matters more than love. Julian is more than ready to sign on for a little superficial dating and a marriage of convenience if it allows him to take his company to the next level. What he wasn't ready for was the woman who shows up as his prospective bride.

Holly Abbott has spent her whole life coming in second. Being born four minutes behind her twin sister has defined her life. But when her headstrong sister refuses to go along with their father's plan to marry her off into a cold business arrangement, Holly has to step up. Knowing the infamous Julian Worth will only entertain marrying the Abbott heir, Holly sets her identity aside to transform into her sister. It's an easy enough plan. A few dates with a man who isn't hers won't hurt anyone.

Except Julian is nothing like the ruthless tycoon she expected. Soon she's left to wonder, what will happen when her sister comes back and worse, how will she ever be able to give up a man who doesn't even know her real name?

Tropes: Enemies to Lovers, Forbidden Love/Off Limits, Marriage of Convenience, Mistaken Identity, Opposites Attract

Genre: Contemporary

Enemies to Lovers Scenario – Marriage of convenience

The heroine's father plans to marry her sister off into a cold business arrangement with the hero but her sister refuses so the heroine steps in to take her place by assuming her sister's identity.

Billionaire Blackmail

By Alison Aimes

After a childhood spent on the streets, ruthless billionaire Nik Valenti has had his share of dealing with crooks. He thought that was behind him. Then five million dollars goes missing...and he knows exactly who stole it. Now, with pride, money, and his company's survival at stake, he won't rest until the beautiful con artist has experienced his own brand of justice.

Sara Turner is no angel, but she's worked hard to prove she's not like her family. Then she's accused of embezzling millions. Worse, the sexy billionaire wants answers. And he's come up with a foolproof way to ensure he gets them. One Sara must accept if she doesn't want to end up in jail.

They might be enemies, but the passion between them is all-consuming, and each time Nik peels away a layer, he discovers there's more to Sara than first meets the eye. He's willing to put everything on the line to find the truth...except his heart.

Tropes: Enemies to Lovers, Opposites Attract, Redemption

Genre: Contemporary

Enemies to Lovers Scenario – Blackmail

When five million dollars goes missing the hero thinks he knows exactly who stole it—the heroine—and he makes her sign a contract whereby she agrees to do whatever he wants or she and her brother will go to jail.

Bite My Fire

By Mary Hughes

Elena O'Rourke packs a gun and an attitude. The gun, because she's a cop. The attitude? Let's just say her love life has been sorely lacking. But she'll be damned if apartment manager Bo Strongwell is going to be the guy to turn that around, despite his Viking warrior vibe, cannonball muscles, and black satin voice—because Bo's the biggest suspect in her murder investigation.

Master vampire Bo Strongwell needs a cop snooping around like he needs a garlic body wash. Fighting rogue vampires keeps him busy enough without Elena suspecting him of murder—even if she smells and tastes like his deepest desires.

Tropes: Enemies to Lovers, Mistaken Identity

Genre: Paranormal

Enemies to Lovers Scenario – Opposite sides of the law

The heroine is a cop and the hero is her biggest suspect in a murder investigation.

Blackmailing the Bad Girl

By Nina Croft

Cynical CEO, Nik Masterton, believes he's finally met a woman who isn't interested in his money...until she vanishes with a hefty amount of it. He's been searching for her ever since and has finally found her doing a stint in Holloway prison for stealing...from someone else. Clearly, he's just one of many. Now she's coming out, and it's time for a little payback.

After two years in prison, Summer Delaney is determined she's never going back. While she had good reasons for doing what she did, it's time to move on to a new life and earn an honest living. Unfortunately, there's a glitch in her plan, and he's waiting at the gate as she comes out.

Nik isn't above using blackmail to make Summer work for him until he decides just how he'll get his revenge. But this time they're both determined to keep their distance. Right until the inconvenient attraction explodes between them...

Tropes: Enemies to Lovers, Blackmail, Boss and Employee, Opposites Attract, Revenge, Second Chance

Genre: Contemporary

Enemies to Lovers Scenario – Revenge

The heroine stole money from the hero and then disappeared. He's been searching for her and finds her in prison for stealing from someone else, so he blackmails her into being his personal assistant to get his revenge.

Blame It on the Bet

By L. E. Rico

Welcome to Mayhem, Minnesota, where the cats wear sweaters, the local priest dispenses dating advice, and you can find your fortune in the bottom of a pie tin.

When her family's pub is threatened with foreclosure, Hennessy O'Halloran, along with her three sisters, is determined to raise enough money to keep it out of the hands of the LA real-estate developer trying to raze it and replace it with a—God forbid!—multiplex theatre.

Bryan Truitt always gets what he wants. And what he wants is the sweet corner property on Mayhem's Main Street where O'Halloran's Pub sits. But his "quick business" turns into more than he bargains for when he meets the feisty Hennessy. Next thing he knows, he's betting her he can outlast Mayhem's punishing winter in time to make the pub his—or he'll gift it to her for free.

Hennessy knows better than to flirt with the enemy. But suddenly Bryan's not sure which he wants more...the property or the woman who owns it.

Tropes: Enemies to Lovers, Bet/Dare/Wager, Opposites Attract

Genre: Contemporary

Enemies to Lovers Scenario – Business takeover

The hero is a real-estate developer and he wants the land the heroine's family pub sits on for a multiplex theatre he's planning. Facing the threat of foreclosure, the heroine and her three sisters are determined to raise enough money to keep it out of his hands, so the heroine makes a bet with the hero.

Brazilian Capture

By Carmen Falcone

Financier turned activist Emanuel Duarte has promised he would find the one witness who can testify against real estate developer Silas Lancaster. Sick of having every attempt at exposing Silas shut down, Emanuel wants to honor a promise he made, and takes from his opponent what matters most—his beautiful daughter Erika. Only he gets more than he bargained for with the tempting—and frustrating—woman.

Fundraiser and socialite Erika Lancaster can't believe she's been kidnapped. Her sexy captor is feeding her lies about her father that she refuses to swallow. Emanuel's plans will hurt her and ruin her mother's legacy—and that she can't allow. Desperate to find a way out of the lush Brazilian jungle, she decides there's only way to disarm the enemy—seduce him.

But her plan backfires and soon she realizes that seducing the enemy comes with a hefty price...loving the enemy simply isn't an option.

Tropes: Enemies to Lovers

Genre: Mystery and Suspense

Enemies to Lovers Scenario – Captured/Kidnapped

The hero is an activist who needs to find a witness who can testify against a real estate developer so he kidnaps the developer's daughter. The heroine can't believe the lies she's being told about her father and she can't allow the hero to ruin her mother's legacy, but to escape the jungle she's imprisoned in she has to seduce the hero.

Captured Heart

By Heather McCollum

Fleeing with only her bow, horse, enormous pet wolf, and the cryptic clues hidden in her mother's medicine journal, healer Meg Boswell gallops north towards freedom, running from the man who falsely accused her mother of witchcraft. Cursed with magical healing abilities, Meg knows that if she's captured, she will die like her mother—atop a blazing witch's pyre.

Winter winds rip across the Highlands, pressing Chief Caden Macbain forward in his desperate plan to save his clan. He's not above using an innocent woman to bargain for peace if it keeps his clan from starving. But Meg isn't who Caden thinks she is, and when she kills a man to save the clan, he must choose between duty and her life. For although he captured her to force a peace, Meg's strength and courage have captured Caden's heart.

Tropes: Enemies to Lovers, Blackmail, Overcoming Odds

Genre: Historical

Enemies to Lovers Scenario – Captured/Kidnapped

Fleeing from the man who falsely accused her mother of witchcraft, the heroine is captured by the hero who plans on using her to bargain with another clan for his own clan's survival.

Catching the CEO

By Victoria Davies

There's nothing quite like being trapped with the one man you can't stand...

Caitlyn Brooks can't believe her luck when her biggest rival turns up at an out of town conference she's attending. CEO of the company threatening to take hers down, she wants nothing to do with Damien Reid or his billions. But the man behind the boardroom is so much more than she imagined.

Damien can barely believe it when Caitlyn shows up at the conference reception. He has no desire to spend a moment longer with the headstrong woman than he has to. Except he can't seem to stop his eyes from following her or the unnerving need to ruffle her perfect feathers. When teasing turns to touching, he's not sure if it's the best or worst mistake of his life.

There's no denying their companies are on a collision course and their hearts might not survive the fallout.

Tropes: Enemies to Lovers, Forbidden Love/Off Limits, Opposites Attract

Genre: Contemporary

Enemies to Lovers Scenario – Business rivals/Competing against each other

The hero and heroine are business rivals—the hero's company is threatening to take hers down. When they both attend an out-of-town conference the hero can't stop the urge to tease the headstrong heroine and ruffle her feathers.

Chasing the Runaway Bride

By Susan Meier

When Marine-turned-rancher, Cade Donovan, inherits his grandfather's grocery store, he has no choice except to return home. A couple of problems with that:

1) The small, gossiping town still doesn't know the real reason Cade left twelve years ago.

2) For some reason, his grandfather added an unexpected detail to the will – Cade has to share ownership with Piper O'Riley.

The O'Rileys and the Donovans have been at each other's throats ever since Cade's grandfather won the store in a poker game. And now Cade has to share his inheritance with the enemy? The gorgeous, tempting, all-grown-up enemy...

After ditching two fiancés at the altar, Piper's earned a reputation as the town's runaway bride. Ironically, Piper is woefully inexperienced with men. Her attraction to Cade and working side-by-side with him is torture. By day, it's non-stop-bickering, but at night, she can't stop imagining all the delicious things Cade could teach her.

With the family grudge and the secret of why Cade really left town between them, there's no way they could ever be together. Right?

Tropes: Enemies to Lovers, Forced Proximity

Genre: Contemporary

Enemies to Lovers Scenario – On opposite sides

The hero and heroine's families have been at each other's throats ever since the hero's grandfather won the grocery store in a poker game. Now they are joint owners of this grocery store since the hero's grandfather left it to them both.

Claiming the Highlander's Heart

By Lily Maxton

Georgina Townsend has never behaved like a "proper" lady. Her family accuses her of being impulsive, sometimes to the point of recklessness. And they must be right. Because when a band of Highland outlaws steals Georgina's late mother's music box, instead of letting the proper authorities take care of the matter she disguises herself as a Highland lass and joins the group of outlaws to find the stolen item. She certainly doesn't plan on falling for their charming leader...

Malcolm Stewart has never met a more bold and captivating woman than the mysterious lass who suddenly shows up to join his small band of outlaws. But while she fits in easily, she's more distracting than he expected. When he returned from the war to find his life destroyed, Mal decided to get revenge on the Highland landlords, whom he blames for the death of his family. Falling in love isn't part of that plan—especially not with the sister of one of the very landlords he's sworn to fight against.

Tropes: Enemies to Lovers, Opposites Attract, Redemption,

Revenge

Genre: Historical

Enemies to Lovers Scenario – On opposite sides

The heroine disguises herself as a Highland lass and joins a group of outlaws to find a stolen item—but she's the sister of the enemy the hero has sworn to fight against.

Coach Maddie and The Marine

By Blaire Edens

After the combat death of her Marine husband, grief counselor Maddie Westerfield has thrown herself into helping other families—leaving no time for dating. Which is just fine with Maddie since falling in love again, especially with another man in uniform, is out of the question. No matter how gorgeous he is. Plus, she's busy looking after her eight-year-old nephew for her deployed sister.

For the last eight years, Lieutenant David Sterling has lived with the guilt of losing one of his soldiers in an ambush in Afghanistan. So when the opportunity presents itself, he jumps at the chance to help the beautiful widow coach her nephew's football team. But keeping things strictly professional between them is harder than he expected. And even though he knows a relationship with Maddie will only lead to heartbreak, he can't help falling for her.

Tropes: Enemies to Lovers, Forced Proximity

Genre: Contemporary

Enemies to Lovers Scenario – Resentment

Years after her husband was killed in combat the heroine meets the hero—the man who'd been her husband's commanding officer.

Cowboys Need Not Apply

By Robert Tate Miller

No, prima donna ballerina Jessica Carmichael isn't interested in the rough-and-tumble rodeo cowboy she met in physical therapy. In fact, she's actively uninterested in his cocky smile, and his go-with-the-flow attitude, and how his silly little bets make her work harder than ever to fix her knee. She'd like nothing more than to strangle him, if she wasn't so busy thinking about kissing him.

Matt Walker's best hope of getting back in the saddle is charming Jessica into teaching him ballet. He needs to get back on the bronc...even if he has to get there in tights. Only the uptight ballerina lives in a completely different world, one he wouldn't touch with a ten-foot mechanical bull. But maybe the one thing she needs more than control is to lose control for once—with him.

Tropes: Enemies to Lovers, Fish Out of Water, Opposites Attract, Overcoming Odds, Redemption

Genre: Contemporary

Enemies to Lovers Scenario – Clash of personalities

The hero and heroine are both in physical therapy but the heroine, a prima donna ballerina, wants nothing to do with the rodeo cowboy hero. Despite this, the hero's working hard to charm this uptight ballerina because he needs her help getting back in the saddle.

Crazy for the Competition

By Cindi Madsen

The road to trouble is paved with sweet temptation...

Always the rebel in her ultra-conservative family, Quinn Sakata dreams of quitting her dad's real-estate business and restoring the old Mountain Ridge Bed and Breakfast in her hometown of Hope Springs. Except that Quinn's not the only person bidding on it. Worse still, her competitor is her high school crush, Heath Brantley, who is all kinds of ripped, tattooed hotness...

So much for her "nice, conservative boys" rule.

Heath has his own reasons for bidding on Mountain Ridge, and he won't give in without a fight—even to the red-lipped hottie with a sailor's mouth. But when their rivalry shifts into an unexpected zing of chemistry, Heath realizes he's in deep trouble. Because it's inevitable that emotions will get involved, and he needs to keep his eyes on the prize before they both get hurt.

Tropes: Enemies to Lovers, Across the Tracks, Opposites

Attract

Genre: Contemporary

Enemies to Lovers Scenario – Business rivals/Competing against each other

Both the hero and the heroine are bidding on the same property because she wants to restore it as a bed and breakfast while he wants to turn it into a hunting lodge. They are the only two people interested in the property and must work together on a project for the town to help the committee make a decision on who wins it.

Dare to Resist

By Laura Kaye

Trapped and tempted, this battle of wills rages all night long...

Kady Dresco and Colton Brooks click on a level that defies logic. There are only two problems. One, he's her older brother's irritating best friend, and two, they're bidding on the same military security services contract.

When the competition heats up, Colton is torn between wanting to strangle Kady (and her annoying brilliance) and kissing her into submission. Which is a bad idea for a million reasons, because Kady's submission is exactly what he craves. Being trapped in a tiny motel room with the object of his darkest fantasies will require every ounce of his restraint.

Kady doesn't want his restraint, but Colton knows better. She deserves love, marriage, and a white picket fence—three things Colton can't give her. But her proximity and the memory of their steamy near-miss three years ago slowly destroys his resolve. And he's not sure how much longer he can keep his hands off...or his heart closed.

Tropes: Enemies to Lovers, Best Friend's Little Sister, Forced Proximity, Second Chance

Genre: Contemporary

Enemies to Lovers Scenario – Business rivals/Competing against each other

The hero and heroine are both bidding on the same military security services contract.

Dirty Games

By Samanthe Beck

A five figure fee. A private villa at an exclusive tropical paradise. Absolute compliance. Top tier celebrity trainer Luke McLean demands all of the above, plus strict adherence to his zero bullshit policy. Especially when faced with six short weeks to whip a spoiled starlet into leading lady shape.

Quinn Sheridan suddenly has half the time she anticipated to turn herself into an action hero for the role of her career. Luckily, her agent calls in a secret weapon, but the demanding, drop dead gorgeous hardass fails to understand SHE'S the client. She has no problem taking direction, but Luke's definition of cooperation feels more like complete and utter submission. And she's tempted to give it to him...

Tropes: Enemies to Lovers, Forced Proximity, Opposites Attract

Genre: Contemporary

Enemies to Lovers Scenario – Clash of personalities

The heroine is an actress who needs to suddenly turn herself into an action hero for the role of her career. Thankfully her agent has just the man for the job, although too bad he sees her as a spoiled starlet.

Distracting the Duke

By Elizabeth Keysian

He's the last thing she wants. She's the last thing he needs.

Devonshire, England, 1820

Determined to avoid the strife-filled marriage of his parents, Marcus, the Duke of Ulvercombe, wants an amenable, biddable wife, and has set his cap for a certain pretty miss. Unfortunately, her vastly opinionated, frustrating, and lamentably beautiful guardian, Lady Clara Tinniswood, keeps distracting him, tempting him to consider a far more tempestuous—and passionate—union.

Recently widowed Lady Clara Tinniswood wants only to organize a quiet new life for herself, beyond the control of any man. But one shockingly unguarded moment while confronted by Marcus's gloriously naked body catapults her headlong into a forbidden passion and threatens to undermine all her well-laid plans.

Even if Marcus abandons his sweet ideal and surrenders to his growing desire for Clara, there's one unalterable issue which could destroy their hopes forever...

Tropes: Enemies to Lovers

Genre: Historical

Enemies to Lovers Scenario – Clash of personalities

The hero is looking for an amenable, biddable wife and has decided on a young lady he considers to be suitable. Unfortunately her guardian—the opinionated, frustrating and beautiful heroine—is tempting him to consider a different union.

Drakon's Knight

By N. J. Walters

Drakon Jericho Drake, the child of a pure-blood dragon and human, has a simple plan: Kill the leader of the Knights of the Dragon and start a war. Except, when he meets his target, Karina Azarov, she can't remember who she is. Worst of all––he can't kill her. His dragon side has just claimed the dangerous woman as his mate.

Karina has no idea why these Drakons have taken her to their home. And she most certainly does not understand why she's so drawn to her captor. Maybe because he's strong, intelligent, and caring, in his enigmatic sort of way. One thing she knows, he's not going to hurt her. If only she could remember something from her past that would explain why these Drakons hate her so much.

But if her memory returns, mated or not, he may get his war.. And one of them will die.

Tropes: Enemies to Lovers, Forced Proximity, Opposites Attract

Genre: Paranormal

Enemies to Lovers Scenario – On opposite sides

The hero is a Drakon, a child of a pure-blood dragon and a human, and he's planning on killing the leader of the Knights of the Dragon, who just happens to be the heroine. But when he meets her he can't kill her because his dragon side has just claimed her as his mate.

Duchess by Day, Mistress by Night

By Stacy Reid

Georgiana Rutherford, the Duchess of Hardcastle, seemingly has it all—wealth, pedigree, and the admiration of the ton, except her heart hungers for a passionate affair. She meets the enigmatic and ruthless Mr Rhys Tremayne, a man known to low and high society as the Broker. The attraction between them is impossible to deny, but she cannot be feeling it for this man.

Rhys Tremayne has built his wealth and empire by dealing secrets on the black market of the London underworld. He is determined to take his sisters away from the depraved world they've known their entire lives, and the duchess is the perfect woman to help sponsor his sisters into society. The only problem is that he wants more from Georgiana, even if the social divide between them ensures she can only ever be his lover in secret.

Tropes: Enemies to Lovers, Accidental Pregnancy, Across the Tracks, Bodyguard/Protector, Fling, Forbidden Love/Off Limits, Redemption

Genre: Historical

Enemies to Lovers Scenario – On opposite sides

The heroine is a duchess and the hero trades in secrets on the black market. When these two meet, the hero decides having a relationship with the heroine will help him sponsor his sisters into society.

Enchanting the Earl

By Lily Maxton

She's the last thing he expected to find...

Llynmore Castle is the only place Annabel Lockhart has ever considered home. For years, she's been able to live as she wished, freely roaming the wild moors. Now there's a new earl, as arrogant as he is handsome, and he wants her out. But if he thinks she'll go quietly, he's in for a surprise.

Theo Townsend returned from war a changed man. After unexpectedly inheriting an earldom and a secluded castle in the Scottish Highlands to go with it, he thinks he's found the perfect place to hide from the world—until he arrives to find a spirited, beautiful woman already in residence. He can't just throw her out, but surely there's a way to get her to leave on her own. The sooner she's gone, the better, especially when he realizes there's more than just mutual dislike between them.

Tropes: Enemies to Lovers, Forced Proximity, Opposites Attract

Genre: Historical

Enemies to Lovers Scenario – Resentment

The hero unexpectedly inherits an earldom and a castle in the Scottish Highlands where he plans on living with his three younger siblings, but he arrives to find a spirited and beautiful woman already in residence with her aunt. He wants the two women to leave as soon as possible so he starts organising them a replacement living situation, but the heroine has other ideas.

Falling for her Enemy

By Victoria James

She's falling for the one man who could destroy everything...

Alex McAllister always dreamed of a life filled with the laughter and love of a family, but being abandoned at a young age left her wary of letting anyone in. Now that she's settled in Still Harbor, Alex struggles between keeping her distance and the magnetic pull of the handsome stranger who claims he's the biological father of her adopted daughter.

Hayden Brooks never wanted to be a father. Long hours spent building his family's real estate empire suits him just fine. But when he discovers an ex put the baby he unknowingly fathered up for adoption, his world crumbles. He tracks the child to Still Harbor with the intention of bringing her home-and comes face to face with his daughter's stunning adoptive mother.

The paternity test is in. And Hayden's about to make the most shocking decision of his life, just in time for Christmas...

Tropes: Enemies to Lovers, Baby on the Doorstep

Genre: Contemporary

Enemies to Lovers Scenario – Resentment

The heroine has a settled life with her adopted daughter but a handsome stranger arrives in town claiming that he's her daughter's biological father, and his intention is to take the baby home with him.

Falling for the Bad Girl

By Nina Croft

It takes an incredibly good man to tame a bad, bad girl...

As a second-generation detective, Nathan Carter is a cop, through and through, one who definitely sees things in black and white. But his work ethic—and libido—are thrown off balance when he heads up the case against jewel thief, Regan Malloy. Because with one sizzling look, she's got him hot and hard. And he's been that way, ever since.

Growing up, Regan's favorite hobby was learning to crack safes, and she was very, very good at it. Still, she'd always tried to keep to the straight and narrow, and only strayed when she believed a friend was in desperate straits. Now she's out of prison and starting over. If only she could forget that she'd spent the last three years fantasizing about the stunningly gorgeous detective who locked her away.

It's inevitable that they meet up again—in bars, hotels...and hotel beds. Despite their differences, they can't keep their hands off each other. Still, it's just desire. If they give it enough time, it'll burn itself out. Because a good boy and a bad girl can't possibly make it work. Can they?

Tropes: Enemies to Lovers, Bad Girl/Rich Boy, Bodyguard/Protector, Opposites Attract, Redemption

Genre: Contemporary

Enemies to Lovers Scenario – Opposite sides of the law

The hero is a detective who worked on a case against a jewel thief—the heroine. She's now out of prison and they've inevitably met up again.

Falling for the Enemy

By Samanthe Beck

Caught between a rock and a rock-hard body...

Salon owner Virginia Boca has declared herself celibate...at least until she wins the election for mayor of Bluelick, Kentucky. No hot men. No sex. And her plan to play the good girl might have worked—if the mysterious, hard-bodied stranger she's seen around town hadn't pulled her from the street and saved her life. The least Ginny can do is offer her savior a free haircut.

But when an innocent haircut turns into hours of wickedly hot sex, former Navy SEAL Shaun Buchanan knows his plan to keep a low profile is shot. Especially once Ginny finds out he's the current mayor's son. With her reputation and the election on the line, Ginny seems determined to keep their nightly sexcapades a secret, but Shaun's not willing to stay in the shadows forever...

Tropes: Enemies to Lovers

Genre: Contemporary

Enemies to Lovers Scenario – On opposite sides

The heroine owns a hairdressing salon and she's also running for mayor. When the hero saves her life their relationship soon includes lots of hot sex, but the heroine has declared herself celibate until after the election and now she's found out her bedpartner is the current mayor's son.

Flirting with the Competition

By Kerri Carpenter

Under normal circumstances, Whitney March might have appreciated sharing an elevator with a ridiculously attractive and clearly wealthy guy. Even enjoyed it. But when her companion turns out to be the man who almost ran her over in the parking garage moments earlier? Nope and nope. Besides, she's on her way to a job interview at a prestigious law firm, and she needs to stay focused. Not staring at the rich and sexy jerk.

Then the elevator comes to an abrupt stop. They're stuck.

Jordan Campbell has every intention of acing the interview for his dream job, and he's not about to let anything stop him. Not even the sexy, capable, and fiery woman who turns out to be his main competitor he's trapped with. The only thing they have in common is determination to get the job...and an escalating attraction. And it's only a matter of time before these competitors indulge in a very sexy little connection between floors.

Tropes: Enemies to Lovers, Bad Girl/Rich Boy, Forced Proximity, One-Night Stand, Opposites Attract

Genre: Contemporary

Enemies to Lovers Scenario – Business rivals/Competing against each other

The hero and heroine are both interviewing at a prestigious law firm for the same job—but when the elevator they're sharing comes to an abrupt stop they indulge in a little sexy connection.

Gilded Lily

By Staci Hart

They say there's no such thing as perfect.

But I've built my life to perfection—the perfect boyfriend, the perfect apartment, the perfect career planning celebrity weddings. My job—my only job—is to make sure every event is absolutely and completely perfect.

What's not perfect? Kash Bennet.

And I wish I didn't find that so appealing.

I could have told you every perfectly imperfect thing about the gardener at Longbourne. Like his hair, lush and black and far too long. Or his nose, the flat bridge of a Greek god, bent a little like it's been broken. Or his size. Beastly. Roped and corded with muscles, gleaming with sweat and peppered with dirt. There's no escaping him, not if I'm going to use his family's flower shop for my events.

But nothing is what it seems. And in the span of a heartbeat, my perfect life is turned inside out. They say the best way to get over somebody is to get under somebody new. When Kash offers his services to the cause, it sounds like the perfect plan.

What's not part of the plan? Falling in love with the gardener.

But they were right—there's no such thing as perfect.

And I'm the fool who finds out the hard way.

Tropes: Enemies to Lovers, Opposites Attract

Genre: Contemporary

Enemies to Lovers Scenario – Clash of personalities
   The hero is the easy-going, go-with-the-flow gardener who works at his family's flower shop. The heroine is career focussed, highly strung and works hard at her job as a wedding planner—and she is going to use the flower shop for her events. Despite their differences, while working closely for a wedding they have fun and seem to bring out the best in each other.

Hard to Protect

By Incy Black

Special Agent Will Berwick doesn't give a damn what his orders are; he's not seducing the lovely but arctic Dr Angel Treherne. Oh, he'll root out her secrets, but on his own terms. Covertly. No compromise.

Caught up in a tangled web of deceit and betrayal, Angel trusts no one—certainly not alpha-cocky, cunning Will Berwick. First he's hostile, then he's charming. Why? What's he hiding? With her life on the line, she needs to know. Preferably without losing her heart in the process.

Tropes: Enemies to Lovers, Bait and Switch, Blackmail, Fish out of Water, Forbidden Love/Off Limits

Genre: Mystery & Suspense

Enemies to Lovers Scenario – On opposite sides

The hero is a special agent whose orders are to seduce the heroine to gain information about her missing brother.

Her Enemy Protector

By Avery Flynn

Enemies can make the most tempting lovers...

By-the-book secret agent Lucas Bendtsen will do anything to keep his country safe—even if that means blackmailing the stepdaughter of a notorious mobster who is about to sell guns to a group of terrorists. The plan? He'll pose as her fiancé in order to access her stepfather's guarded compound and find out the location of the arms deal. The problem? Despite her reputation as a heartless femme fatale, Ruby Macintosh is not at all what she seems.

Only a fool would double-cross the Organization, but Ruby doesn't have any choice—not if she's going to save her brother and mother from her stepfather. So she places her life in the hands of a man who turns her on as much as he ticks her off...

The fake engagement may be the beginning of a high-stakes game of subterfuge, but when their hearts get involved, Lucas has to decide whether to break the rules or break Ruby's heart.

Tropes: Enemies to Lovers, Bodyguard/Protector, Fake Engagement

Genre: Contemporary

Enemies to Lovers Scenario – On opposite sides

The heroine's father is about to sell guns to a group of terrorists and the hero, a secret agent, plans to use his daughter to find out the location of the arms deal. But the heroine needs to save her brother and mother from her stepfather, so the hero finds she's willing to double-cross her father to do so.

His Pirate Seductress

By Tamara Hughes

A woman of passion. A man of principle. And only one can win...

With her son's life in the balance, Catherine Fry is forced to locate and steal the priceless Ruby Cross of the Knights Templar. She knows who has it – it's just a matter of coercing Thomas Glanville, the handsome and incredibly stubborn captain of the ship she's captured, into telling her the exact location. Fortunately, Catherine knows that there are many ways to get a man to talk...

Captain Thomas Glanville has the cross and he'll be damned if he's going to hand it over now that he finally has the means to buy a ship of his own. He's at the mercy of a fiery woman who will stop at nothing to achieve her goal. But Catherine has no idea who she's dealing with – and Thomas has his own means of charming a woman into his mercy and his bed...

Tropes: Enemies to Lovers, Forced Proximity

Genre: Historical

Enemies to Lovers Scenario – Captured/Kidnapped

The heroine is a pirate and in order to protect her son she is forced to locate and steal the priceless Ruby Cross of the Knights Templar. She's captured the hero because she knows he has the cross and now it is just a matter of getting him to talk. But the hero needs the cross to buy a ship of his own.

His Rebellious Lass

By Callie Hutton

He wants to marry her off quickly. She says absolutely not.

When the Marquess of Campbell inherits a fiery, red-headed Scottish beauty as his ward, it's his job to marry her off. No problem. She comes with a fortune. Lady Bridget MacDuff will have suitors falling all over themselves to wed her.

Not so fast. Lady Bridget has plans for that fortune and they involve helping unfortunate women. And she has no intention of helping her devastatingly handsome guardian in his quest to get her off his hands. He doesn't plan to marry, either. Why should she?

Bridget and Cam are now on opposite sides of a war that neither one plans to lose. Even if Cam's rakish presence throws Bridget's heart into turmoil and the marquess can't deny that his ward sets his heart afire. And then Cam makes a bold proposal...

Tropes: Enemies to Lovers, Bodyguard/Protector, Forced

Proximity, Opposites Attract, Overcoming Odds

Genre: Historical

Enemies to Lovers Scenario – Clash of personalities
   When the hero inherits the heroine as his ward it's his job to marry her off. But the heroine has no intention of marrying and so they engage in a battle of wills.

His Undercover Princess

By Avery Flynn

Protecting her is his job...whether she wants him to or not.

Stylist Elle Olsen lives in fear of someone discovering her secret identity as Princess Eloise. But the men who killed her entire family in a bloody coup have done just that and now they're coming for her. All Elle wants is to disappear into anonymity again, but the panty-melting billionaire who kidnaps her isn't about to let that happen.

On the society pages, smoking hot financier Dominick Rasmussen is one of the world's most eligible bachelors, but there's more to him than meets the eye. As a secret resistance fighter, his one goal is to get Princess Eloise on the throne and restore the monarchy. The biggest problem? His stubborn and sexy undercover princess has no interest in ever wearing a tiara again.

Their goals couldn't be more opposed, but neither Dom nor Elle can deny the attraction bringing them closer together. As the stakes rise and danger increases, they are forced to choose between love and country...

Tropes: Enemies to Lovers, Bodyguard/Protector, Forced Proximity, Royalty

Genre: Contemporary

Enemies to Lovers Scenario – On opposite sides

When the heroine's secret identity as a princess is discovered she needs to disappear again because the men who killed her entire family are now coming for her. But the hero, a secret resistance fighter, wants her on the throne to restore the monarchy. As they fight opposing goals the danger increases and so does the attraction between them.

How to Best a Marquess

By Tina Gabrielle

When a handsome boxer kisses Lady Ellie Swift for good luck during a match, it turns her world upside down. Because the rogue isn't just anyone...it's the Devil Marquess returned. Thanks to Hugh Vere, Marquess of Deveril, Ellie learned at an early age that men are more trouble than they're worth. Now, instead of a husband, she wants to take over her brother's infamous gambling club—the Raven Club. And apparently the devil wants it, too.

From the moment Hugh sees Ellie again sparks fly, but battle lines have been drawn. Whoever is the most successful overseeing the club in one month's time will win. And Hugh intends to win. And he intends to stay very close to Ellie to make sure she follows the rules. What he discovers, though, is that Ellie is no longer the sweet girl he knew years ago—and winning won't be easy. But the nearly combustible chemistry between them is hard to ignore, and soon the club is not the only prize he wants...

Tropes: Enemies to Lovers, Bet/Dare/Wager, Reunited Lovers

Genre: Historical

Enemies to Lovers Scenario – Business rivals/Competing against each other

   The heroine wants to take over her brother's infamous gambling club and so does the hero. They decide on a wager—whoever is the most successful at overseeing the club in one month's time will win. But the hero finds out that the heroine isn't the sweet girl he knew years ago.

How to Bewitch an Earl

By Ally Broadfield

He never expected the clues to lead to her...

Edward Adair, heir to the Duke of Boulstridge, is more interested in finding a missing family heirloom than a wife. But
when his parents issue an ultimatum – marry or lose your
allowance – he reluctantly agrees to attend a house party to
find a bride. Instead, he discovers attractive but infuriating
Miss Isabella Winthrop in his library, reading the private family
journal that holds clues to the location of the heirloom.

Though Isabella finds Edward haughty and arrogant, she offers
to take him to the next clue mentioned in the journal if he
will pay her, which will enable her to help her brother restore
his estate. Edward counters with an offer of an even larger
payment...if she agrees to masquerade as his betrothed to deter
the other ladies until the house party ends.

As they work together to solve the mystery their mutual
attraction grows, but just when they begin to think they should
make their engagement real, a secret is revealed that could

destroy everything.

Tropes: Enemies to Lovers, Fake Engagement

Genre: Historical

Enemies to Lovers Scenario – On opposite sides

The hero and heroine are both after the hero's missing family heirloom. The hero has also been given an ultimatum by his parents that he needs to find a bride, so they come to an arrangement—she will pretend to be his betrothed at the house party they're both attending and he will give her money to help restore her brother's estate.

How to Play the Game of Love

By Harmony Williams

He's everything she thinks she doesn't want.

When Miss Rose Wellesley's father threatens an arranged marriage, she knows she'd better settle on a choice quickly or end up having no say in who she marries. Fortunately, she's garnered a rare invitation to Lady Dunlop's "Week of Love" house party, an annual affair notorious for matchmaking. Her plans to expedite a proposal would go smoothly if not for the brash younger sister she must chaperone, her outspoken, disagreeable best friend, and the bullish Lord Hartfell who seems determined to dog her every step.

Lord Hartfell embodies every last thing Rose dislikes in a man. He's domineering, tenacious, argumentative, and a little too casual with his nudity for her tastes. Worst of all, Rose can't seem to get him—or his kisses—out of her mind.

Rose is determined to find a more appropriate husband, even if her heart disagrees with how unsuitable the stubborn lord is...

Tropes: Enemies to Lovers

Genre: Historical

Enemies to Lovers Scenario – Clash of personalities
The heroine's father has threatened her with an arranged marriage so she decides to find herself a husband at a house party she's been invited to—but the hero seems determined to hinder her progress.

Impulse Control

By Amanda Usen

Sign: Aries

He's fiery, courageous...and he can't resist a sexy challenge.

Survivalist Russ Donovan is known on TV as the "Wildest Man In The World." The last thing this headstrong Aries guy needs is to be wrangled into a cross-promotional TV special with a popular homemaker—even a sexy little thing like Susannah Stone. Besides, the Adirondacks in the dead of winter is no place for amateurs...especially a stubborn homemaker who's determined to show him up every chance she gets.

Susannah's a working single mom who knows plenty about roughing it. She can take anything this mountain man dishes out. Now Russ and Susannah are taking their competitive rivalry to new levels, and not even the canned beef stew is safe. Then Russ and Susannah's on-camera sparks turn into a sizzling off-camera romance, and their two conflicting worlds collide.

Sure, major differences can turn chemistry red-hot...they also make compromise nearly impossible.

Tropes: Enemies to Lovers, Co-workers, Opposites Attract

Genre: Contemporary

Enemies to Lovers Scenario – Clash of personalities

The hero is a survivalist and he's strong-armed into filming a new television show with the heroine who's a lifestyle expert. She may be a homemaker but that doesn't mean the heroine can't handle anything the mountain man dishes out.

Kissing her Crush

By Ophelia London

Chocolate makes you happy. It might as well be a universal truth, especially in Hershey, Pennsylvania, and chocolate chemist Natalie Holden intends to prove it. She might not be lucky in love, but if she can show her chocolate recipe helps teenage depression it will make everything worth it. There's just one sexy problem—Luke Elliot, the guy she's had a crush on since birth, is the microbiologist set to debunk her study. And, of course, he looks more delicious than ever!

Luke doesn't believe this project has a leg to stand on, so he's shocked to discover Natalie heading it. His "what if" girl from high school, she's still as tempting as he remembers. Especially when she's daring him to taste test chocolate and arguing with him over every possible thing. The late nights in the lab definitely don't help. They may not see eye-to-eye on her project, but they can't deny the explosive chemistry that keeps pulling them together. Even when it risks their jobs and the very different futures they both want...

Tropes: Enemies to Lovers, Co-workers, Opposites Attract

Genre: Contemporary

Enemies to Lovers Scenario – On opposite sides
The heroine is a chocolate chemist and intends to prove that her chocolate recipe helps teenage depression, but the hero, a microbiologist, is set to debunk her study.

London Calling

By Veronica Forand

Small town police officer Emma Ross loves her simple life--but it takes a hard turn into crazy when she's kidnapped by MI6 and is put under the protection of an over-bearing, albeit sexy, Scotsman. A man who believes she's lying to protect her father—a father whom she had no idea worked for British Intelligence and is now missing.

Liam Macknight's partner was assassinated and he's certain Emma's father had something to do with it. But the stubborn woman isn't talking, and she's determined to get herself killed trying to find out the truth. Locking her in a room does no good--he tried that. So he's forced to work with her, even if he's not sure he'll ever be able to trust her.

When he's assigned to kill her dad to protect the identity of British spies in the Kremlin, he knows what little trust they've gained is about to be destroyed forever...

Tropes: Enemies to Lovers, Bodyguard/Protector, Fish out of Water, Overcoming Odds

Genre: Romantic Suspense

Enemies to Lovers Scenario – Captured/Kidnapped

The heroine, a small-town police officer, is kidnapped by MI6 and put under the protection of the hero. He believes she is lying to protect her father whom he's certain had something to do with his partner's death.

Mistress Spy

By Pamela Mingle

A determined sister...

Madeleine Vernon's dreams should be filled with elegant gowns and marriageable men. Instead, she dreams of avenging her brother's death. But when she's captured by the queen's men, she's forced to become a spy by her mysterious yet undeniably attractive captor.

A rakish spy...

After years of working for his father in Queen Elizabeth's service, Nicholas Ryder is close to going his own way. But now he's got a feisty beauty he must protect or risk her execution as a traitor to the crown. She's a distraction he can't afford, but he also can't stop thinking about her.

A dangerous lie...

It is Nicholas's job to foil plots against Elizabeth, and he sends Maddy into a household of suspected traitors to garner what information she can. As the line between captor and prisoner blurs, deceit, betrayal, and desire become a perilous mix. Ultimately, Nicholas must decide whether duty to the queen is more important than winning Maddy's heart.

Tropes: Enemies to Lovers, Blackmail, Bodyguard/Protector, Boss and Employee, Opposites Attract, Overcoming Odds, Revenge

Genre: Contemporary

Enemies to Lovers Scenario – On opposite sides

While trying to avenge her brother's death the heroine is captured by the queen's men and forced to become a spy by the hero, who's working for his father in Queen Elizabeth's service.

Moonlight

By Lisa Kessler

Embrace your destiny...

Rancher Adam Sloan is more than meets the eye. As the heir to his Pack, the sexy werewolf's biggest challenge is keeping his kin's true nature under wraps. But a group of jaguar shifters threatens to reveal the pack, blasting into town killing humans in plain sight. And when he smells one at the local diner, his standing orders are to take her out.

Lana Turpin doesn't realize she's a moving target. Raised in the foster system, she only knows that she blacks out during the new moon and wakes up without remembering a thing. But now she's being tracked by some strange organization that wants her back—even though she's never stepped foot inside their compound. And the stranger across the diner is watching her like an enemy.

It should be a simple mission for Adam, but when he touches the frustratingly beautiful Lana, his inner wolf howls...mate. Now, the two must find and stop the people who hunt her...and

Adam must keep his own family from killing the only woman he will ever love.

Tropes: Enemies to Lovers, Bodyguard/Protector, Forbidden Love/Off Limits, Opposites Attract

Genre: Paranormal

Enemies to Lovers Scenario – On opposite sides

The hero is heir to a pack of werewolves, and while trying to protect them when a group of jaguar shifters come into town and start killing humans he comes across the heroine at the local diner. The heroine doesn't realise she's a shifter, having been raised in foster care. The heroine should be his enemy, but one touch and he realises she's his mate.

Once in a Blue Moon

By Amanda Ashby

Florist Laney George has a successful business, amazing friends and big, big dreams––oh, and a broken heart. But she's working through that last one. Then the man she hoped to never see again shows up––and Laney's carefully ordered plans are experiencing technical difficulties.

Celebrated Author Adam Fitzpatrick planned to be in St. Clair for no more than a day. Sign the books, and get out. Same story, different day. What he didn't count on was Laney George, who happens to be the star of his somewhat fictional tale. She broke his heart years ago, and he'd gone a bit mad. Okay, maybe a lot mad––and he put everything in his book, never imagining it would be a world-wide best seller.

Now that he's seen her again, he wants answers. But it isn't just her that draws him in. It's the town, something is happening and for the first time in years...he can write again. If only he could convince the woman who hates him most to start a new chapter in their story.

Tropes: Enemies to Lovers, Second Chance

Genre: Contemporary

Enemies to Lovers Scenario – Resentment

   The hero and heroine were in a relationship but broke up, leaving both of them feeling resentful. The heroine moved on and now has a successful business, while the hero, struggling to get over the heroine, put everything into a book which has become a best-seller—and he sees her again while visiting her town to sign copies.

Once Upon a Masquerade

By Tamara Hughes

New York City, 1883

A Prince Charming meets his match...

Self-made shipping magnate Christopher Black first spies Rebecca Bailey at a masquerade ball and is captivated by her refreshing naiveté and sparkling beauty. She's a stark contrast to the hollow behaviour of the ton and the guile of his former fiancee, but the closer he gets to her secrets, the further she pushes him away.

A Cinderella with a secret...

Rebecca is drawn to the charismatic Christopher from the first, but she cannot risk him discovering that she is really a housemaid impersonating an heiress. Her father's life depends on it.

A Happily Ever After that could never be...

When Christopher's investigation of the murder of his best friend leads him straight to Rebecca, he fears his ingenue may be a femme fatale in disguise. Now he must decide if he can trust the woman he's come to love, or if her secrets will be his downfall.

Tropes: Enemies to Lovers, Across the Tracks, Bait and Switch, Fish Out of Water, Forbidden Love/Off Limits

Genre: Historical

Enemies to Lovers Scenario – On opposite sides

The heroine is a housemaid impersonating an heiress because she needs to become a rich gentleman's mistress in order to get money to pay off her father's gambling debts. The hero spots her at a masquerade ball and becomes intrigued by her, but he's also investigating the murder of his best friend which seems to lead straight to the heroine.

Operation Cinderella

By Hope Tarr

Manhattan magazine editor Macie Graham always gets her story—and she'll do anything to uncover the dirt on famous conservative radio personality Ross Mannon. After he smears her article on his show, nearly costing Macie her job, she devises a plan to masquerade as a modern-day Cinderella and get her revenge on the infuriating Texan.

All Ross wants is a woman with old-fashioned values to be his housekeeper and role model for his troubled teenage daughter. When the perfect woman shows up, Ross is relieved—until he finds himself drawn to his gorgeous, red-stiletto-wearing new employee. "Martha Jane" is opinionated and sexy, and Ross is intrigued...and more than a little turned on.

Macie thought Operation Cinderella was foolproof, but Ross, with his rugged good looks and southern charm, proves to be as perfect behind-the-scenes as he does in public. But when she finally uncovers a secret that could destroy Ross's reputation, she faces losing her job or losing the fairy-tale ending she didn't even know she wanted.

Tropes: Enemies to Lovers, Forced Proximity, Revenge

Genre: Contemporary

Enemies to Lovers Scenario – Revenge

When the heroine's magazine article is smeared by the hero on his radio show she nearly loses her job. Determined to find something about him to get her revenge, she masquerades as a modern-day Cinderella and applies for the housekeeper job he is advertising.

Opposing the Cowboy

By Margo Bond Collins

Never trust a good kisser...

Yoga teacher LeeAnn Walker has no desire to see the unspoilt beauty of her grandmother's ranch violated by a greedy oil company. But unless she finds the paperwork confirming she owns the mineral rights, that's exactly what could happen. The worst part? The guy spearheading the whole mess is none other than the hot and sexy stranger LeeAnn just kissed to make her ex jealous.

Jonah Hamilton thought his day was looking up until he found out the gorgeous blonde who kissed the hell out of him is the same stubborn woman he came to town for. And she's not too happy to find out she might be forced to allow drilling on her land.

But Jonah has a job to do, even if LeeAnn tempts him to turn his professionalism into something much more personal...

Tropes: Enemies to Lovers, Forced Proximity, Opposites Attract

Genre: Contemporary

Enemies to Lovers Scenario – Resentment
The heroine must prove that she has the mineral rights to her grandmother's ranch; otherwise she'll be forced to allow the hero to drill on her land.

Playing at Love

By Ophelia London

When it's glee vs gridiron, can love level the playing field?

Show choir teacher Tess Johansson loves three things: music, her job, and sharing that passion with her students. But when a school budget crisis forces funding to be pulled from either the sports or music programs, she finds herself going head to head with Jack, the gorgeous new football coach who broke her heart fifteen years ago.

Jack Marshall wants two things: to be closer to his young daughter and to make his mark as a football coach. Taking the new job, with the promise that he'd have time to build a solid team, gave him both. But now he must win the season with a group of boys who aren't anywhere near ready or he'll lose everything he's worked so hard for. Being pitted against Tess, the summer love he never forgot, is like being fourth and long with only seconds on the clock.

On opposing sides of a fierce battle and with everything at stake, Tess and Jack find themselves torn between doing what it takes to win and doing what it takes to be together.

Tropes: Enemies to Lovers, Opposites Attract, Reunited Lovers, Second Chance

Genre: Contemporary

Enemies to Lovers Scenario – Business rivals/Competing against each other

When the school where she teaches has a budget crisis, the heroine—who's the choir teacher—and the football coach hero must compete for the school's funding.

Prisoner of Love

By Cathy Skendrovich

Risking his own life is one thing. Risking hers is another...

It was supposed to be a girls-only weekend in the California mountains. But when Lucy Parker is carjacked by an escaped prisoner, her fun weekend takes a nightmarish turn. Now she's caught up in a dangerous world of stolen money, vicious drug dealers, and murder, and the only thing keeping her alive is her oh-so-hot captor.

Imprisoned for a crime he didn't commit, undercover cop Jake Dalton wants answers—now. Worse, he's dragged Lucy into the mix, and she's now guilty by association. With their lives on the line, the race is on to get to Las Vegas before they're killed...and they're running out of time.

Tropes: Enemies to Lovers, Forced Proximity, Ugly Duckling

Genre: Romantic Suspense

Enemies to Lovers Scenario – Captured/Kidnapped

When the heroine is carjacked by the hero—an escaped prisoner and ex-undercover cop—she becomes involved in his battle to clear his name while they try to stay alive.

Protecting What's His

By Tessa Bailey

She's running from the law, and the law wants her bad.

The opportunity was just too damn delicious for Ginger Peet to pass up. The purse full of money she finds—$50,000 to be exact—could give her and her teen sister the new start they need. So she grabs the cash, her gothy sibling, and their life-sized statue of Dolly Parton, and blows outta Nashville in a cloud of dust. Chicago, here we come...

Turns out, Chicago has some pretty hot cops. Hot, intense, naughty-lookin' cops like Derek Tyler, who looks like he could eat a girl up and leave her begging for more. And more. Tempting as he is, getting involved with the sexy homicide lieutenant next door poses a teensy problem for a gal who's on the lam. But one thing is certain—Derek's onto her, and he wants more than just a taste.

And as far as he's concerned, possession is nine-tenths of the law.

Tropes: Enemies to Lovers, Bodyguard/Protector, Opposites Attract

Genre: Contemporary

Enemies to Lovers Scenario – Opposites sides of the law

The heroine's mother is a drug addict and gets involved with same really bad people, so when she comes back one night and passes out on the sofa the heroine grabs her mother's purse containing $50,000 in cash, and flees with her sister. They move into an apartment next door to the hero, a homicide lieutenant, who's intent on getting to know her.

Risky Surrender

By Robin Bielman

Lucy Davenport made a promise to her father and husband right before they died and she's vowed to keep it at any cost. But when she draws unwanted attention to her secret plans, she's forced to risk everything she's kept guarded. Because the man standing in her way threatens not only her goal, but the walls she's carefully constructed around her heart.

Keats McCall is an environmental preservationist navigating the globe on behalf of heritage protection. When he catches Lucy at his latest project, he suspects she's up to no good. She's secretive, sexy as hell—and has trouble written all over her. He devises a plan to keep her close so he can keep an eye on her. But what he isn't prepared for is just how close he wants to get.

Tropes: Enemies to Lovers, Bad Boy/Bachelor/Playboy Reformed, Forbidden Love/Off Limits

Genre: Contemporary

Enemies to Lovers Scenario – On opposite sides

The heroine is an archaeologist and the hero an environmental preservationist. They first met when the heroine stole an ancient emerald, so now when the hero finds her at a historic site his company is preserving, he's suspicious and determined to find out what she's up to.

Romancing the Rumrunner

By Michelle McLean

Prohibition Era Chicago

She's worked too hard to be run out of town...

Jessica Harlan spends her nights as The Phoenix, the owner of the most popular speakeasy in town. Her days are spent running her respectable butcher shop and dodging prohibition agents and rival club owners who all want to put her out of business.

He's worked too hard to let his heart get in the way...

When the opportunity arises to go undercover for the Feds to catch The Phoenix, Gumshoe Anthony Solomon jumps on it. But he never suspected the notorious rumrunner would be a dame—or that he'd be so drawn to the feisty little minx.

They play a dangerous game of cat and mouse, knowing they can't trust the other, but unable to walk away. While their hearts dodge the crossfire, the mobsters raise the stakes, and

136

even the Phoenix may not rise again.

Tropes: Enemies to Lovers, Mistaken Identity, Opposites Attract

Genre: Historical

Enemies to Lovers Scenario – Opposite sides of the law

The heroine is a rumrunner in Chicago during the time of prohibition and the hero is an undercover detective determined to catch her.

Running with a Sweet Talker

By Jami Albright

*She's a take-no-prisoners fireball. He's a sweet-talking charmer.
It could be love...if they don't kill each other first.*

Hotshot lawyer Luanne Price may not believe in happily ever
after, but she'd do just about anything to earn her absentee
father's love. So when he waltzes back into her life with a plan
for her to marry his business associate, she foolishly agrees.
But on the wedding day, things go south. Fast. Luanne's
desperate to get away, even if that means hitching a cross-
country ride with the infuriating Jack Avery.

Jack needs to get Luanne out of his system. He'll watch her tie
the knot and forget about her. Once she's married to another
man, then she'll be off-limits forever. Solid plan. Until he spots
her army-crawling through the bushes to escape the Wedding
of the Season.

He knows he should let someone else deal with the runaway
bride. But if there's one thing Jack has never been able to do,
it's resist Luanne. Will their romance rev up on the open road,

or will Jack and Luanne crash and burn?

Tropes: Enemies to Lovers, Forced Proximity

Genre: Contemporary

Enemies to Lovers Scenario – Resentment

The hero and heroine are both successful lawyers and have always been adversaries, picking at each other and inflicting pain whenever they could. But when the heroine needs to escape her wedding because her groom is a cheater, the hero is there to help her escape.

Sins of her Father

By Kathleen Mix

Someone had to make him pay...

Faith Rochambeau is horrified to learn she was conceived during a rape. She's determined to make her biological father, Victor Telemann, pay for his crimes. Using her computer skills to dig into his life, she searches for the powerful man's Achilles Heel and a way to extract retribution. She'll do whatever it takes to get a conviction, even it if means infiltrating his Fortune 500 company.

She fails to plan on falling in love with her father's smooth-talking stepson, Kent Telemann, who suspects she is a corporate spy. Faith is drawn to Kent, even though she's not sure she can trust him. If her heart is wrong, he can put her life in danger.

Meanwhile, her father is playing a lethal game he's determined to win.

Tropes: Enemies to Lovers, Overcoming Odds, Revenge

Genre: Romantic Suspense

Enemies to Lovers Scenario – Revenge

When the heroine learns she was conceived during a rape she's determined to make her biological father pay for his crimes. The hero is her father's stepson and he suspects her of being a corporate spy.

Spiced

By Jamie Farrell and Pippa Grant

Dueling neighbors, baby fever, fake boyfriends, and pizza... Life in Bliss has never been better!

Pepper Blue wants a baby. Forget the husband. She's better at training men to be good husbands for other women than she is at getting one herself, so she's doing this on her own.

But she hasn't exactly shared the news with her family, and they're determined to find her a date to the next family wedding. A date that won't ditch her for one of her sisters or cousins. This time.

Which means Pepper Blue needs a fake boyfriend. A fake boyfriend that she has no chance of actually falling in love with. A fake boyfriend like her obnoxious neighbor.

Tony Cross is a pizza god with a sausage problem. He's putting on a good show—a different woman at his house every night, flirting with all the right customers, flexing his muscles when called upon—but since his divorce, his meat has been more on the undercooked side. If you know what he means.

Except, unfortunately, when it comes to his annoyingly perfect, always put together, too good for him neighbor. Pepper Blue. Who is not a viable candidate for fixing his "little problem."

So he's not sure why he's coming to her rescue, pretending to be her boyfriend to save her from a bad date at his pizza joint. He just knows it's fun. And it irritates her. And it turns out, she might be able to help his flagging pizza sales as much as she's helping his flagging... you know.

So long as this is just business, he's happy to keep pushing her buttons.

All night long, if he has to.

Tropes: Enemies to Lovers, Forced Proximity

Genre: Contemporary

Enemies to Lovers Scenario – Resentment
   The hero and heroine are neighbours—he thinks she is annoyingly perfect and too good for him, while she thinks he's just obnoxious. But she needs a fake boyfriend for a family wedding and he's happy to oblige because it'll be fun pushing her buttons.

Sweet Home Highlander

By Amalie Howard, Angie Morgan

Lady Aisla Montgomery has a perfectly tolerable marriage...as long as her husband stays in Scotland and she in Paris. But now, years later, she wants only one thing—a divorce.

Niall Stuart Maclaren, the rugged Laird of Tarbendale, rues the day he met his beautiful, conniving wife. Though the thought of her incites a bitter and biting fury, no other woman has ever stirred his blood as hotly. When Aisla returns to Scotland to sever ties, Niall agrees on one condition—one week with him for every year of desertion. Six weeks as his wife in his castle...in his bed...in exchange for her freedom.

Tropes: Enemies to Lovers, Bet/Dare/Wager, Blackmail, Forced Proximity, Reunited Lovers, Second Chance

Genre: Historical

Enemies to Lovers Scenario – Resentment
   When the heroine returns to Scotland to sever ties with her estranged husband, he agrees on one condition—one week

with him for every year of her desertion.

Taming the CEO

By Hayson Manning

Falling for the enemy was never in the plan.

To save her family's business, fledging CEO Daisy Cater must win the bid on a resort on St. Maarten. There's a small catch, though. The seller insists all bidders visit the island and experience the singles retreat firsthand. This wouldn't be so bad...if only rule-maker Daisy weren't paired with her bitter rival, the hot and broody Alexander Gillard. Keeping her enemy close just became a whole lot harder.

Alexander "Zan" Gillard didn't expect to be partnered with gorgeous Daisy at the idyllic singles retreat. A challenge that has them cuffed together ignites an explosive chemistry, and soon Zan wants more than four days with this bewitching woman who is nothing like he expected her to be.

But their families are at odds and reality awaits them at home, along with a betrayal that threatens to blow their newfound trust apart...

Tropes: Enemies to Lovers, Bait and Switch

Genre: Contemporary

Enemies to Lovers Scenario – Business rivals/Competing against each other

The hero and heroine both intend on bidding on a resort but the seller has insisted that all bidders must visit the island and experience the singles retreat first-hand. Unfortunately the hero and heroine have been paired up and neither expected the chemistry between them.

Tangled Hearts

By Heather McCollum

Growing up on a pirate ship, every day was full of adventure for Pandora Wyatt. It was also the perfect place for her to use her magic without persecution. But after her surrogate father is imprisoned in the Tower of London, Pandora leaves the safety of the vessel to rescue him before he's executed. She expects her mission to be difficult, but what she doesn't expect is to have her life saved by the sexiest man she's ever met.

Highland warrior Ewan Brody always wanted a sweet, uncomplicated woman by his side, but he can't fight his attraction to the beautiful enchantress who's stumbled into his life. He quickly learns, though, that Pandora is not only a witch, but also a pirate and possibly a traitor's daughter—and though she's tricked him into playing her husband at King Henry's court, he's falling hard.

Soon, they begin to discover dark secrets leading to the real traitor of the Tudor court, the one Ewan was hired to capture. Now, Ewan and Pandora must uncover the truth before they lose more than just their hearts.

Tropes: Enemies to Lovers, Fake Relationship, Marriage of Convenience, Royalty

Genre: Historical

Enemies to Lovers Scenario – On opposite sides
The hero is on a mission to bring a traitor to Henry VIII, while the heroine must save her father who's been imprisoned in the Tower of London for being an alleged traitor to the king. The hero rescues the heroine from certain death as she's about to be executed for being a witch.

Tempting the Corporate Spy

By Angela Claire

He's stealing more than her heart...

Whiz kid Liv Altman is working on Internet anti-piracy soft-ware that could be huge. It could also be dangerous. And someone wants it badly enough to blackmail only the very best hacker—the infamous and reclusive Jonathon Crestwell—into stealing it...

Liv usually has no trouble ignoring the computer geeks she works with every day, but her new corporate consultant is definitely not easy to ignore. He's tall and dead hot, with deep blue eyes that make Liv think the naughtiest of HR-violating thoughts. When she finds him unexpectedly in her office one evening, things take a turn for the sexier. But come morning, Liv will discover the truth about her new employee...and what he really wants.

Tropes: Enemies to Lovers, Boss and Employee, Mistaken Identity

Genre: Contemporary

Enemies to Lovers Scenario – On opposite sides

The hero is a computer hacker and he's being blackmailed into stealing the heroine's anti-piracy software. She hires him as her corporate consultant but unexpectedly finds him in her office one evening.

The Dare

By Lauren Landish

Have you ever had one of those really bad days at work?

You know, one where your hot boss catches you photocopying your backside in his office?

No? Just me then?

I blame my bestie and partner in chaos.

She challenged me with a not-so-innocent dare that I should've flat out declined.

But I'm an adrenaline junkie, and now, here I am.

I know it sounds crazy, and daredevil tendencies aside, I definitely went too far to get his attention.

But you haven't seen him.

Colton Wolfe. My boss.

Tall, dark, and handsome, with the sexiest British accent I've ever heard.

His only flaw? That he's completely oblivious to what's been right in front of him all along.

Me.

Well, he was until a few minutes ago.

Remember those good old days?

Before I got caught making "nice" with the copy machine, and before I was totally getting fired?

But wait. Maybe I'm not.

If I can take on the biggest dare of all.

Making Colton Wolfe fall in love with me.

Tropes: Enemies to Lovers, Co-workers, Forced Proximity

Genre: Contemporary

Enemies to Lovers Scenario – On opposite sides

The heroine works at the company where her father is the vice-president. The hero transfers from the UK to this company because he's looking for better career opportunities. The hero and the heroine's father are both competing for the same position in the company and they each want to use the heroine as leverage against the other. Her father wants her to find gossip on the hero, while the hero has bigger plans for her—so she is struggling with her growing attraction to the hero and her loyalty to her father.

The Duke Meets his Match

By Tina Gabrielle

The daughter of an infamous art forger, Chloe Somerton grew up poor. Desperate to aid her sisters, she'd picked a pocket...or two. Now circumstances have changed, and Chloe has a chance to marry a young, wealthy lord. Only his mentor—a dark, dangerous duke—stands in her way. The duke knows about her past, and she'll do anything to keep him from telling.

The moment Michael Keswick, the Duke of Cameron, sees Chloe Somerton, he recognizes her as a fraud. The stunning beauty with sapphire eyes and golden hair now appears to be a proper lady, but he knows better. What begins as a battle of wills soon escalates into a fierce attraction. In Chloe, Michael finds peace from the memories of war, but he refuses to marry...and she won't settle for anything less.

Tropes: Enemies to Lovers, Forbidden Love/Off Limits

Genre: Historical

Enemies to Lovers Scenario – On opposite sides

The heroine is the daughter of an art forger, and having grown up poor she's picked a few pockets. Now she has the chance to marry a wealthy lord but his mentor, the hero—a dark, dangerous duke—stands in her way because he knows about her past.

The Greek Tycoon's Tarnished Bride

By Rachel Lyndhurst

Sign: Capricorn

He loves power, material success...and sex.

Erica Silver has never done things the "usual" way. A single mom working towards a degree in psychology, she's paying her way as an exotic dancer. No one can tell Erica how to live her life...especially not some handsome, arrogant Greek stranger, who wants to take her son away from his "unfit" mother.

Successful entrepreneur Tito Makris has no choice but to fulfill his best friend's last wish. He must bring his friend's son to Greece to claim a multi-billion euro legacy. Still, taking the boy from his mother—however tarnished she may be—is pretty much the last thing Tito wants. So he offers Erica a radical choice: marry him and stay with her son...or lose the boy—and him—forever.

Tropes: Enemies to Lovers, Fish Out of Water, Marriage of Convenience

Genre: Contemporary

Enemies to Lovers Scenario – Marriage of convenience

The heroine is a single mother studying for a degree in psychology while working as an exotic dancer to pay her way. The hero needs to fulfil his best friend's last wish—to bring his friend's son back to Greece to claim a multi-billion euro legacy. But taking the boy away from his mother isn't what he really wants to do, so he offers the heroine marriage which will mean she can stay with her son—or she'll lose him forever.

The Highlander Who Loved Me

By Tara Kingston

Johanna Templeton is on a life-and-death quest. Swept into an intrigue that rivals the tales she pens, she joins forces with a Highland rogue to find the treasure that will save her kidnapped niece—a prize the Scot seeks for reasons that have nothing to do with ransom. Engaging the Highlander in a sizzling battle of the sexes, Johanna shields her heart.

Connor MacMasters, spy for Queen Victoria, is a man on a mission—keep a legendary gemstone from an evil man. Trailing an American novelist who holds the key to the treasure should've been simple, but Johanna awakens feelings he'd long thought dead. Torn between duty and desire, he wants her in his bed, but loving her would be a fool's game. Blasted shame his heart doesn't agree.

Tropes: Enemies to Lovers, Bodyguard/Protector, Overcoming Odds, Revenge

Genre: Historical

Enemies to Lovers Scenario – On opposite sides

The heroine must find a book that the people holding her niece captive want in return for her niece's release. The hero joins her in the search, but his motives for wanting the book aren't the same as the heroine.

The Hunt

By Harper A. Brooks

For years, tiger and panther shifters have been at odds. And now the tension is higher than ever. A panther shifter is accused of assassinating the tiger shifter king. Prince Kael is determined to find whoever is responsible for his father's murder and make them pay.

With the ceremonial Hunt approaching, he must also focus on finding a mate to run with him.

But when he finds the panther suspect, his inner tiger becomes unleashed. After all these years he's finally found his mate: Cara, a panther...and the main suspect in his father's murder. Despite it all, Kael would do anything to claim her.

The hatred between the tigers and panthers is all their people know. If Kael and Cara follow their hearts, it could mean treason and death.

Tropes: Enemies to Lovers, Forbidden Love/Off Limits, Royalty

Genre: Paranormal

Enemies to Lovers Scenario – On opposite sides

The hero is a tiger shifter and the heroine's a panther shifter—and they are enemies. After the hero's father is assassinated he's determined to find the person responsible, but when he learns that the suspect is the heroine he realises she's the mate he's been looking for.

The Kissing Contract

By Amy Andrews

Marshall Dyson wants one thing and one thing only: to raze his grandfather's island to the ground. Everything is ready to go--except for the freakin' bunnies! Hundreds of the furry critters hopping about and multiplying before his eyes. And then there's the American Bunny League, along with one distractingly beautiful veterinarian, taking him to court to save them...

Dr. Augusta "Gus" North can't believe the grumpy—and annoyingly hot—builder she's facing in court cares more about demo-ing some cabin than the lives of 200 bunnies. But when the judge orders Marshall to stay on the island and help her rehome the rabbits – the entire month – she knows they're going to need to lay some ground rules.

Like, for example, absolutely no kissing. Might as well go ahead and get that in writing. Sure it's on a napkin, but that still counts.

How hard could it be to keep their hands off each other amidst all the fighting? Surprisingly, harder than wrangling 200 bunnies...

Tropes: Enemies to Lovers, Across the Tracks, Forced Proximity, Opposites Attract

Genre: Contemporary

Enemies to Lovers Scenario – On opposite sides

The hero and his brother have inherited their grandfather's property which is an island in the middle of a lake. Previously no one was able to visit the island but they want to open it up to families by building cabins and changing it from private use to public. To get started they want to burn off everything on the island but the problem is that there are hundreds of rabbits living on the island. The heroine is a veterinarian and she is taking the hero to court to save the rabbits. The judge has ordered that the two of them must stay on the island and rehome the bunnies.

The Last Second Chance: A Small Town Love Story

By Lucy Score

What would it take to get one last chance?

Joey Greer is done having her heart broken. Eight years ago, after a horrific car accident, Jackson Pierce—her high school sweetheart—abandoned her. Abandoned his family. Abandoned the town they'd both grown up in, and fled to Hollywood. He never looked back, and she never forgot him.

Or forgave him.

Now he's back, pretending like the past doesn't exist, wanting another chance. And even though she still feels the undeniable connection between them, the fiery attraction that burns her up from the inside out, Joey's determined to keep him at a safe distance.

Jackson Pierce can't tell Joey the truth about the night when he left her in the hospital. It would ruin more than just their relationship, and he can't do that to her.

The entire town of Blue Moon knows that Jax and Joey are meant for each other, but Joey isn't interested in giving him a second chance. All he can do is give her flowers. And picnic lunches. And a dog.

Oh, and handcuff himself to her for charity.

Will this second chance be the last one Jax needs to win back Joey's heart, or is the past too much to forgive?

Tropes: Enemies to Lovers, Forced Proximity, Second Chance

Genre: Contemporary

Enemies to Lovers Scenario – Resentment

The hero and heroine were high school sweethearts, but while she was in the hospital recovering from a horrific car accident he abandoned her and his family, and left town. Now he's back and pretending the past never happened—but he can't tell her what really happened because that would ruin more than just their relationship.

The Millionaire's Forever

By Sonya Weiss

Sign: Gemini

There are two sides to every Gemini guy...and one of them is red-hot.

Olivia Carter has a handsome, millionaire boyfriend. She's madly in love with him. The hitch? He doesn't actually exist. She told the lie to save Forever, her wedding design shop. And it worked—almost too well. As the media attention increases, so do the demands for Olivia to produce her "boyfriend." With both her reputation and career in jeopardy, Olivia is desperate enough to do almost anything...

Which is exactly what millionaire Mason Parker wants. Thanks to Olivia and her father, Mason went through hell during his teen years, and now it's time for a little payback—starting with the announcement that he's her one and only. Now the sexy Olivia has no choice but to do what Mason wants. But none of his plans for vengeance included falling in love with the woman he planned to ruin...

Tropes: Enemies to Lovers, Fake Relationship, Revenge

Genre: Contemporary

Enemies to Lovers Scenario – Revenge

The hero and heroine knew each other in high school—he was considered a bad boy and she was the sheriff's daughter. The heroine has no memories of an event in their past that saw the hero and his friends being sent to a juvenile correctional facility where horrible things happened to them. Now he's made something of his life he's out for revenge against her father and wants him to answer for what happened. He also wants the land the juvenile facility stands on because he wants to burn it to the ground, but the heroine owns it. So when the heroine's wedding design business is in jeopardy if she can't produce a fictional boyfriend she's been pretending to have he comes to her rescue—though he's going to blackmail her at the same time.

The Playboy's Proposal

By Ashlee Mallory

Sometimes the perfect match is right under your nose...

Doctor Benny Sorensen has had it up to here with her party-throwing playboy neighbor. She's declaring war. She doesn't care how gorgeous or charming he is, he's going down. That is until he proposes something she's not sure she can say no to...

Wealthy ad man Henry Ellison lives an uncomplicated life that revolves around work, women, and partying. In that order. Until Benny storms into his life. To placate his attractive but hotheaded neighbor, Henry offers to help her land a date with the man of her dreams. Only as Henry makes her over and coaches her on the fine art of flirting, he realizes that the idea of this woman in any other man's arms but his own is unacceptable.

But Benny's a forever kind of girl and forever might just be the one commitment he can't make.

Tropes: Enemies to Lovers, Ugly Duckling

Genre: Contemporary

Enemies to Lovers Scenario – Clash of personalities

The heroine is totally fed up with her party-throwing playboy neighbour and she's about to declare war—but the hero offers to help her land a date with the man of her dreams.

The Scottish Rogue

By Heather McCollum

1684, Scottish Highlands

Clan chief Grey Campbell would rather die than see Finlarig Castle, his family home, fall into English hands. He's already had to fight off a blazing fire, likely set by the outsiders constantly lurking outside the castle, so one beautiful Englishwoman flashing a bill of sale does not intimidate him.

Evelyn Worthington has dreams her own. Dreams that could finally come true, now that her brother has purchased a Scottish castle. The trek from England was exhausting, but it will all be worth it once she can get past the brawny Highlander and into her castle... And ignore the passions that flare between them.

It's a battle of wills, but Evelyn and Grey aren't the only ones with their sights set on Finlarig. As secrets are revealed and muskets are lit, the fate of the Campbell Clan, Evelyn's hard-fought plan, and the possible future between this Sassenach and Highlander are in as much jeopardy as their lives.

Tropes: Enemies to Lovers, Opposites Attract, Overcoming Odds, Political Scandal, Revenge

Genre: Historical

Enemies to Lovers Scenario – Resentment

The heroine, an Englishwoman, is resolved to build a school for ladies in her brother's Scottish castle. But when she arrives she finds the castle scorched by fire and a brawny Highlander barring her entry. As the clan chief, the hero would rather die than see his family home fall into English hands—even if the heroine does have a bill of sale.

Torch in the Forest

By Marcie Kremer

Eleanor of Strathcombe is stunned to realize she has a powerful attraction to Hugh of Wykeham, the arrogant, neighboring lord returned from the Crusade. But he wants to marry her sister, and when he learns that poachers are running rampant he blames her and feuds with her over the control of their forest boundaries. As she struggles to keep control of her forests and find the poachers, unsettling feelings confront her when she deals with Hugh, feelings she never felt in her brief, loveless marriage.

When she finds herself in the midst of a net of intrigue and lies, she needs to find the courage to capture the conspirators, save herself and her sister, and overcome her feelings for Hugh...even though that's the last thing she wants to do.

Tropes: Enemies to Lovers

Genre: Historical

Enemies to Lovers Scenario – Clash of personalities

The heroine works hard to take care of her younger sister and her late husband's estates. But when her arrogant neighbour, the hero—who wants to marry her sister—blames her for poachers running rampant they argue over the control of their forest boundaries.

Totally, Sweetly, Irrevocably

By Kira Archer

Their sexy stakeout will turn his orderly world upside down...

When Officer Rick Boyd answers a call about a peeping Tom, he doesn't expect to find a gorgeous woman holding the binoculars. But Gina Silvano's no peeping Tom, and she can catch her cupcake truck's kinky vandals herself, thank you very much. No sexy cops required.

No matter how hot their stakeouts, by-the-book Officer Boyd can't see a future with a dangerous, rule-breaking wild-child who despises the law. He's never felt more alive, though, and expunging her from his heart might be impossible.

But loving each other might cost them more than they are able to give.

Tropes: Enemies to Lovers, Opposites Attract

Genre: Contemporary

Enemies to Lovers Scenario – Opposite sides of the law

The hero is a police officer, and when he is called out to investigate a peeping Tom he doesn't expect to find a woman is the culprit. But the heroine is out to catch whoever's vandalising her cupcake van and she doesn't need his help.

What a Scot Wants

By Amalie Howard, Angie Morgan

Highlander Ronan Maclaren must marry, but he's in no particular hurry. He's perfectly happy as the laird of his clan, running the Maclaren Whisky Distillery, and besides, he just hasn't found the right woman.

Lady Imogen Kincaid has cleverly avoided wedlock for years. Men, she has learned from painful experience, are not to be trusted. Determined to remain independent, she takes an indecent amount of pleasure in making herself as unattractive to potential suitors as possible.

When desperate measures are taken by their parents and a betrothal contract is signed, it's loathing at first sight. They each vow to make the other cry off—by any means necessary. But what starts out as a battle of wits...quickly dissolves into a battle of wills.

Tropes: Enemies to Lovers, Arranged Marriage, Bet/Dare/Wager, Bodyguard/Protector, Fake Relationship, Opposites Attract, Overcoming Odds

Genre: Historical

Enemies to Lovers Scenario – Resentment

The hero is a Highland duke and he's dedicated to leading his clan and maintaining their whiskey distillery. The heroine has avoided marriage and is determined to maintain her independence and her inheritance, which she uses to support a charitable women's shelter she's set up. When the hero's father's will stipulates an ultimatum that forces them to become betrothed neither of them is happy about it. But for both of them, something they hold dear is at stake if they back out—so they each try to get the other to cry off.

Wicked in his Arms

By Stacy Reid

Tobias Walcott, the Earl of Blade, has learned it is best to exercise rigid control over his passions and emotions in all that he does. Uncaring that it makes him seem cool and aloof to most in the ton, he is content with his desire to only woo agreeable and demur females. Then unforeseen circumstances see him trapped in a closet at a house party with the last woman he would ever make his countess.

Lady Olivia Sherwood is everything he should not desire in a female—unconventional, too decisive, and utterly without decorum. But passion ignites between them and they are discovered. Honor demands they wed, and while Tobias finds himself unwillingly drawn to the bewitching beauty, he must do everything not to tempt the passion that burns in him for her, lest it leads to disastrous consequences.

Tropes: Enemies to Lovers, Accidental Marriage, Forced Proximity, Opposites Attract

Genre: Historical

Enemies to Lovers Scenario – Clash of personalities

The heroine is the daughter of a Baron whose suicide led to scandal. Her mother remarries but when the heroine's stepfather takes ill he beseeches her to go to his cousin so that she can be groomed for the upcoming season. He wants her to be married and protected before his son inherits. So she does as he wishes and goes to his cousin's house to be tutored in being a perfect lady. This is where she meets the hero, who is extremely conservative and loathes scandal or behaviour unbecoming a lady, and he immediately thinks very poorly of her. Too bad they end up in a closet together and when discovered by his mother are forced into marriage to stop the gossips.

Your B&B or Mine

By Melissa West

All's fair in love and war, especially in the Deep South...

Savannah Hale never planned to come back to Maple Cove, Georgia. Her hometown has too many painful memories, especially of her high school sweetheart, who was killed during combat. And yet here she is...broken-hearted from her mother's death and left to deal with the Hale family legacy—Maple Cove's landmark bed and breakfast. In need of repairs and near foreclosure, she's hanging on to the B&B by a thread.

And the man out to buy it is the man she's never been able to forgive...or forget.

Former soldier Logan Park is haunted by memories of his own. Some are of his best friend. Others are filled with longing for the girl he could never have. Now Savannah is back, and their attraction can't be denied. But Logan has already sacrificed everything to atone for his sins, and there's no way he'll let himself fall for a girl who might never love again.

Tropes: Enemies to Lovers, Forbidden Love/ Off Limits, Second Chance, Unrequited Love

Genre: Contemporary

Enemies to Lovers Scenario – On opposite sides

The heroine returns to her hometown after the death of her mother. She plans to take over the family legacy and run the B&B, but she doesn't realise it is actually in financial trouble. The hero was the best friend of her deceased boyfriend and he also works for the company that's wanting to take over the B&B.

Plot Scenarios for Enemies to Lovers

The following is a list of the situations, or reasons, the enemies to lovers trope has been used in these stories. I've grouped them into categories of common themes, although some stories may fit into more than one theme; in these cases I've chosen the one I think is the best fit with the story's plot.

Blackmail

Billionaire Blackmail
When five million dollars goes missing the hero thinks he knows exactly who stole it—the heroine—and he makes her sign a contract whereby she agrees to do whatever he wants or she and her brother will go to jail.

Business rivals/Competing against each other

Besting the Billionaire
The hero and heroine are competing for the position of CEO of the same company.

Catching the CEO
The hero and heroine are business rivals—the hero's com-

pany is threatening to take hers down. When they both attend an out-of-town conference the hero can't stop the urge to tease the headstrong heroine and ruffle her feathers.

Crazy for the Competition

Both the hero and the heroine are bidding on the same property because she wants to restore it as a bed and breakfast while he wants to turn it into a hunting lodge. They are the only two people interested in the property and must work together on a project for the town to help the committee make a decision on who wins it.

Dare to Resist

The hero and heroine are both bidding on the same military security services contract.

Flirting with the Competition

The hero and heroine are both interviewing at a prestigious law firm for the same job—but when the elevator they're sharing comes to an abrupt stop they indulge in a little sexy connection.

How to Best a Marquess

The heroine wants to take over her brother's infamous gambling club and so does the hero. They decide on a wager—whoever is the most successful at overseeing the club in one month's time will win. But the hero finds out that the heroine isn't the sweet girl he knew years ago.

Playing at Love

When the school where she teaches has a budget crisis, the

heroine—who's the choir teacher—and the football coach hero must compete for the school's funding.

Taming the CEO

The hero and heroine both intend on bidding on a resort but the seller has insisted that all bidders must visit the island and experience the singles retreat first-hand. Unfortunately the hero and heroine have been paired up and neither expected the chemistry between them.

Business takeover

Blame It on the Bet

The hero is a real-estate developer and he wants the land the heroine's family pub sits on for a multiplex theatre he's planning. Facing the threat of foreclosure, the heroine and her three sisters are determined to raise enough money to keep it out of his hands, so the heroine makes a bet with the hero.

Captured/Kidnapped

Brazilian Capture

The hero is an activist who needs to find a witness who can testify against a real estate developer so he kidnaps the developer's daughter. The heroine can't believe the lies she's being told about her father and she can't allow the hero to ruin her mother's legacy, but to escape the jungle she's imprisoned in she has to seduce the hero.

Captured Heart

Fleeing from the man who falsely accused her mother of

witchcraft, the heroine is captured by the hero who plans on using her to bargain with another clan for his own clan's survival.

His Pirate Seductress

The heroine is a pirate and in order to protect her son she is forced to locate and steal the priceless Ruby Cross of the Knights Templar. She's captured the hero because she knows he has the cross and now it is just a matter of getting him to talk. But the hero needs the cross to buy a ship of his own.

London Calling

The heroine, a small-town police officer, is kidnapped by MI6 and put under the protection of the hero. He believes she is lying to protect her father whom he's certain had something to do with his partner's death.

Prisoner of Love

When the heroine is carjacked by the hero—an escaped prisoner and ex-undercover cop—she becomes involved in his battle to clear his name while they try to stay alive.

Clash of personalities

A Millionaire at Midnight

The hero overhears the heroine saying that she's on the hunt for a rich man who's good in the sack and thinks she's just another gold digger. Things go from bad to worse when she wins a date with him at a bachelor auction and then he discovers she's the executive assistant at the company he's just acquired. Later, in exchange for him giving her the money she needs to help save a charity close to her heart, she agrees to a fake engagement with him because he needs a fiancée to cement a position with his family company.

A Rogue for Emily

The hero and heroine have never liked each—she thinks he is sexist towards her, and he finds she never has anything kind to say to him. But they are paired up for a mission so have no choice but to spend time together.

An Accidental Date with a Billionaire

When the heroine accidentally bids on the wrong CEO at a charity auction she's about to call the whole thing off but the hero insults her—so now she's hatching a plan to put him right in his place.

Armed 'N' Ready

The hero is after a major illegal gun dealer and his best lead is the heroine but she's not cooperating. The heroine's business is in jeopardy due to the hero's suspicion that she's involved, so the only way to get him off her back is to cooperate.

Asking for Trouble

The hero and heroine have mutual friends which means they often end up being in the same room but that only brings out the worst in them—a dislike for each other is just the starting point, until their explosive arguments end up in a night of mind-blowing sex. But the heroine must marry the son of a wealthy CEO to secure a deal and prevent her father's company from financial ruin; however the hero has other ideas.

At the Spy's Pleasure

The heroine is putting together a list of gentlemen she thinks will be suitable as a lover, although she's most definitely not putting the hero's name on her list since he's far too arrogant in her opinion. The hero is masquerading as an arrogant barrister to conceal his real occupation of a spy, and one of his suspects is on the heroine's list—giving him a good reason to keep her in his bed where she'll be safe.

Bad Mouth

The hero is a cocky vampire who's been tasked with helping the heroine solve a slew of murders. The heroine is well-bred and on the serious side so she's annoyed with the hero's crass language and blunt way of saying things.

Cowboys Need Not Apply

The hero and heroine are both in physical therapy but the heroine, a prima donna ballerina, wants nothing to do with the rodeo cowboy hero. Despite this, the hero's working hard to charm this uptight ballerina because he needs her help getting back in the saddle.

Dirty Games

The heroine is an actress who needs to suddenly turn herself into an action hero for the role of her career. Thankfully her agent has just the man for the job, although too bad he sees her as a spoiled starlet.

Distracting the Duke

The hero is looking for an amenable, biddable wife and has decided on a young lady he considers to be suitable. Unfortunately her guardian—the opinionated, frustrating and beautiful heroine—is tempting him to consider a different union.

Gilded Lily

The hero is the easy-going, go-with-the-flow gardener who works at his family's flower shop. The heroine is career focussed, highly strung and works hard at her job as a wedding planner—and she is going to use the flower shop for her events. Despite their differences, while working closely for a wedding they have fun and seem to bring out the best in each other.

His Rebellious Lass

When the hero inherits the heroine as his ward it's his job to marry her off. But the heroine has no intention of marrying and so they engage in a battle of wills.

How to Play the Game of Love

The heroine's father has threatened her with an arranged marriage so she decides to find herself a husband at a house party she's been invited to—but the hero seems determined to hinder her progress.

Impulse Control

The hero is a survivalist and he's strong-armed into filming a new television show with the heroine who's a lifestyle expert. She may be a homemaker but that doesn't mean the heroine can't handle anything the mountain man dishes out.

The Playboy's Proposal

The heroine is totally fed up with her party-throwing playboy neighbour and she's about to declare war—but the hero offers to help her land a date with the man of her dreams.

Torch in the Forest

The heroine works hard to take care of her younger sister and her late husband's estates. But when her arrogant neighbour, the hero—who wants to marry her sister—blames her for poachers running rampant they argue over the control of their forest boundaries.

Wicked in his Arms

The heroine is the daughter of a Baron whose suicide led to scandal. Her mother remarries but when the heroine's stepfather takes ill he beseeches her to go to his cousin so that she can be groomed for the upcoming season. He wants her to be married and protected before his son inherits. So she does as he wishes and goes to his cousin's house to be tutored in being a perfect lady. This is where she meets the hero, who is extremely conservative and loathes scandal or behaviour unbecoming a lady, and he immediately thinks very poorly of her. Too bad they end up in a closet together and when discovered by his mother are forced into marriage to stop the gossips.

Heroine feels unfairly treated by the hero

69 Million Things I Hate About You

The heroine is the hero's personal assistant and she feels he places ridiculous demands on her, expecting her to be available 24/7 for whatever whim he demands. When she and her friends win the lottery, instead of quitting her job she decides to exact a little satisfying revenge by deliberately being terrible at her job.

When the hero finds out there's an office pool on how long it will take him to fire her he decides to join the fun. But as sparks fly between them their irritation with each other crosses the line into something quite different.

A Man of Honor

The hero and heroine kept in contact via Skype while he was overseas fighting in the war, but he breaks contact with her after he gets wounded. When he returns to town to attend a wedding, she wants answers.

Interference by others

A Mistress for Penndrake

The hero is being blackmailed into marrying the heroine—someone he's never met—in order to get back the ancestral home his father gambled away. Annoyed at being dictated to, he decides to ruin the woman he's being forced to marry, but he soon realises she isn't the sort of woman one can ruin without consideration. The blackmailer has regrets over his actions and warns the heroine about the hero. Not knowing the details regarding the warning, she decides to keep clear of the hero at all costs. But no matter how hard this couple try to dislike each other their mutual attraction can't be suppressed.

Beauty and the Werewolf

The hero is an unmated werewolf who needs a mate to stay alive. When he sees the heroine he wants her because he recognises she's the one—his fated mate—but their packs are enemies. The heroine already struggles with gaining her father's approval, and falling in love with the hero makes that even harder.

Marriage of convenience

Betraying the Billionaire

The heroine's father plans to marry her sister off into a cold business arrangement with the hero but her sister refuses so the heroine steps in to take her place by assuming her sister's identity.

The Greek Tycoon's Tarnished Bride

The heroine is a single mother studying for a degree in psychology while working as an exotic dancer to pay her way. The hero needs to fulfil his best friend's last wish—to bring his friend's son back to Greece to claim a multi-billion euro legacy. But taking the boy away from his mother isn't what he really wants to do, so he offers the heroine marriage which will mean she can stay with her son—or she'll lose him forever.

On opposite sides

Chasing the Runaway Bride

The hero and heroine's families have been at each other's throats ever since the hero's grandfather won the grocery store in a poker game. Now they are joint owners of this grocery store since the hero's grandfather left it to them both.

Claiming the Highlander's Heart

The heroine disguises herself as a Highland lass and joins a group of outlaws to find a stolen item—but she's the sister of the enemy the hero has sworn to fight against.

Drakon's Knight

The hero is a Drakon, a child of a pure-blood dragon and a human, and he's planning on killing the leader of the Knights of the Dragon, who just happens to be the heroine. But when he meets her he can't kill her because his dragon side has just claimed her as his mate.

Duchess by Day, Mistress by Night

The heroine is a duchess and the hero trades in secrets on the black market. When these two meet, the hero decides having a relationship with the heroine will help him sponsor his sisters into society.

Falling for the Enemy

The heroine owns a hairdressing salon and she's also running for mayor. When the hero saves her life their relationship soon includes lots of hot sex, but the heroine has declared herself celibate until after the election and now she's found out her bedpartner is the current mayor's son.

Hard to Protect

The hero is a special agent whose orders are to seduce the heroine to gain information about her missing brother.

Her Enemy Protector

The heroine's father is about to sell guns to a group of terrorists and the hero, a secret agent, plans to use his daughter to find out the location of the arms deal. But the heroine needs to save her brother and mother from her stepfather, so the hero finds she's willing to double-cross her father to do so.

His Undercover Princess

When the heroine's secret identity as a princess is discovered she needs to disappear again because the men who killed her entire family are now coming for her. But the hero, a secret resistance fighter, wants her on the throne to restore the monarchy. As they fight opposing goals the danger increases and so does the attraction between them.

How to Bewitch an Earl

The hero and heroine are both after the hero's missing family heirloom. The hero has also been given an ultimatum by his parents that he needs to find a bride, so they come to an arrangement—she will pretend to be his betrothed at the house party they're both attending and he will give her money to help restore her brother's estate.

Kissing her Crush

The heroine is a chocolate chemist and intends to prove that her chocolate recipe helps teenage depression, but the hero, a microbiologist, is set to debunk her study.

Mistress Spy

While trying to avenge her brother's death the heroine is captured by the queen's men and forced to become a spy by the hero, who's working for his father in Queen Elizabeth's service.

Moonlight

The hero is heir to a pack of werewolves, and while trying to protect them when a group of jaguar shifters come into town and start killing humans he comes across the heroine at the local diner. The heroine doesn't realise she's a shifter, having

194

been raised in foster care. The heroine should be his enemy, but one touch and he realises she's his mate.

Once Upon a Masquerade

The heroine is a housemaid impersonating an heiress because she needs to become a rich gentleman's mistress in order to get money to pay off her father's gambling debts. The hero spots her at a masquerade ball and becomes intrigued by her, but he's also investigating the murder of his best friend which seems to lead straight to the heroine.

Risky Surrender

The heroine is an archaeologist and the hero an environmental preservationist. They first met when the heroine stole an ancient emerald, so now when the hero finds her at a historic site his company is preserving, he's suspicious and determined to find out what she's up to.

Tangled Hearts

The hero is on a mission to bring a traitor to Henry VIII, while the heroine must save her father who's been imprisoned in the Tower of London for being an alleged traitor to the king. The hero rescues the heroine from certain death as she's about to be executed for being a witch.

Tempting the Corporate Spy

The hero is a computer hacker and he's being blackmailed into stealing the heroine's anti-piracy software. She hires him as her corporate consultant but unexpectedly finds him in her office one evening.

The Dare

The heroine works at the company where her father is the vice-president. The hero transfers from the UK to this company because he's looking for better career opportunities. The hero and the heroine's father are both competing for the same position in the company and they each want to use the heroine as leverage against the other. Her father wants her to find gossip on the hero, while the hero has bigger plans for her—so she is struggling with her growing attraction to the hero and her loyalty to her father.

The Duke Meets his Match

The heroine is the daughter of an art forger, and having grown up poor she's picked a few pockets. Now she has the chance to marry a wealthy lord but his mentor, the hero—a dark, dangerous duke—stands in her way because he knows about her past.

The Highlander Who Loved Me

The heroine must find a book that the people holding her niece captive want in return for her niece's release. The hero joins her in the search, but his motives for wanting the book aren't the same as the heroine.

The Hunt

The hero is a tiger shifter and the heroine's a panther shifter—and they are enemies. After the hero's father is assassinated he's determined to find the person responsible, but when he learns that the suspect is the heroine he realises she's the mate he's been looking for.

The Kissing Contract

The hero and his brother have inherited their grandfather's property which is an island in the middle of a lake. Previously no one was able to visit the island but they want to open it up to families by building cabins and changing it from private use to public. To get started they want to burn off everything on the island but the problem is that there are hundreds of rabbits living on the island. The heroine is a veterinarian and she is taking the hero to court to save the rabbits. The judge has ordered that the two of them must stay on the island and rehome the bunnies.

Your B&B or Mine

The heroine returns to her hometown after the death of her mother. She plans to take over the family legacy and run the B&B, but she doesn't realise it is actually in financial trouble. The hero was the best friend of her deceased boyfriend and he also works for the company that's wanting to take over the B&B.

Opposite sides of the law

A Lady Never Tells

The heroine is a spy working for His Majesty's personal homeland network and she's been tasked with infiltrating high society to uncover enemies—with the hero's family being at the top of her list.

Bite My Fire

The heroine is a cop and the hero is her biggest suspect in a murder investigation.

Falling for the Bad Girl

The hero is a detective who worked on a case against a jewel thief—the heroine. She's now out of prison and they've inevitably met up again.

Protecting What's His

The heroine's mother is a drug addict and gets involved with same really bad people, so when she comes back one night and passes out on the sofa the heroine grabs her mother's purse containing $50,000 in cash, and flees with her sister. They move into an apartment next door to the hero, a homicide lieutenant, who's intent on getting to know her.

Romancing the Rumrunner

The heroine is a rumrunner in Chicago during the time of prohibition and the hero is an undercover detective determined to catch her.

Totally, Sweetly, Irrevocably

The hero is a police officer, and when he is called out to investigate a peeping Tom he doesn't expect to find a woman is the culprit. But the heroine is out to catch whoever's vandalising her cupcake van and she doesn't need his help.

Resentment

A Moment of Madness

The heroine returns home to find out her father has passed away and his bar now belongs to the hero. They are both resentful and wary of each other, but the heroine wants the opportunity to work at the place that meant so much to her father and the hero is desperate for a waitress.

A Pirate's Command

The hero is a pirate and he's married to the heroine, but she can't continue to live as the wife of a pirate so she returns to her family, taking their son with her. When someone kidnaps their child they blame each other—however they'll need to work together to find him.

A Vengeful Affair

The heroine believes the hero was responsible for the demise of her best friend so she's going to make him pay by sabotaging the merger he's working on.

Awakening: Britton

The hero feels resentment towards the heroine because she took his job as head of the SPAC; meanwhile the heroine dislikes the hero's attitude, and his flagrant flirting and bedding of women. Now they have to team up on a high-stakes ransom case which requires them to spend several days together in a cabin in the mountains.

Coach Maddie and The Marine

Years after her husband was killed in combat the heroine meets the hero—the man who'd been her husband's commanding officer.

Enchanting the Earl

The hero unexpectedly inherits an earldom and a castle in the Scottish Highlands where he plans on living with his three younger siblings, but he arrives to find a spirited and beautiful woman already in residence with her aunt. He wants the two women to leave as soon as possible so he starts organising them a replacement living situation, but the heroine has other ideas.

Falling for her Enemy

The heroine has a settled life with her adopted daughter but a handsome stranger arrives in town claiming that he's her daughter's biological father, and his intention is to take the baby home with him.

Once in a Blue Moon

The hero and heroine were in a relationship but broke up, leaving both of them feeling resentful. The heroine moved on and now has a successful business, while the hero, struggling to get over the heroine, put everything into a book which has become a best-seller—and he sees her again while visiting her town to sign copies.

Opposing the Cowboy

The heroine must prove that she has the mineral rights to her grandmother's ranch; otherwise she'll be forced to allow the hero to drill on her land.

Running with a Sweet Talker

The hero and heroine are both successful lawyers and have always been adversaries, picking at each other and inflicting pain whenever they could. But when the heroine needs to escape her wedding because her groom is a cheater, the hero is there to help her escape.

Spiced

The hero and heroine are neighbours—he thinks she is annoyingly perfect and too good for him, while she thinks he's just obnoxious. But she needs a fake boyfriend for a family wedding and he's happy to oblige because it'll be fun pushing her buttons.

Sweet Home Highlander

When the heroine returns to Scotland to sever ties with her estranged husband, he agrees on one condition—one week with him for every year of her desertion.

The Last Second Chance: A Small Town Love Story

The hero and heroine were high school sweethearts, but while she was in the hospital recovering from a horrific car accident he abandoned her and his family, and left town. Now he's back and pretending the past never happened—but he can't tell her what really happened because that would ruin more than just their relationship.

The Scottish Rogue

The heroine, an Englishwoman, is resolved to build a school for ladies in her brother's Scottish castle. But when she arrives she finds the castle scorched by fire and a brawny Highlander barring her entry. As the clan chief, the hero would rather die than see his family home fall into English hands—even if the heroine does have a bill of sale.

What a Scot Wants

The hero is a Highland duke and he's dedicated to leading his clan and maintaining their whiskey distillery. The heroine has avoided marriage and is determined to maintain her independence and her inheritance, which she uses to support a charitable women's shelter she's set up. When the hero's father's will stipulates an ultimatum that forces them to become betrothed neither of them is happy about it. But for both of them, something they hold dear is at stake if they back out—so they each try to get the other to cry off.

Revenge

An Artful Seduction
The hero is the enemy of the heroine's father, and he seeks justice for the art forger having duped half the ton. He blackmails the heroine into helping him find her father so he can turn the man in—if she refuses he'll ruin her.

Beauty and the Bachelor
The hero is seeking revenge against the heroine's father and decides to use the heroine as bait. He blackmails her into marriage by threatening to expose her father's shady business dealings.

Blackmailing the Bad Girl
The heroine stole money from the hero and then disappeared. He's been searching for her and finds her in prison for stealing from someone else, so he blackmails her into being his personal assistant to get his revenge.

Operation Cinderella
When the heroine's magazine article is smeared by the hero on his radio show she nearly loses her job. Determined to find something about him to get her revenge, she masquerades as a

modern-day Cinderella and applies for the housekeeper job he is advertising.

Sins of her Father

When the heroine learns she was conceived during a rape she's determined to make her biological father pay for his crimes. The hero is her father's stepson and he suspects her of being a corporate spy.

The Millionaire's Forever

The hero and heroine knew each other in high school—he was considered a bad boy and she was the sheriff's daughter. The heroine has no memories of an event in their past that saw the hero and his friends being sent to a juvenile correctional facility where horrible things happened to them. Now he's made something of his life he's out for revenge against her father and wants him to answer for what happened. He also wants the land the juvenile facility stands on because he wants to burn it to the ground, but the heroine owns it. So when the heroine's wedding design business is in jeopardy if she can't produce a fictional boyfriend she's been pretending to have he comes to her rescue—though he's going to blackmail her at the same time.

List of Stories by Genre

Contemporary

69 Million Things I Hate About You
  A Man on Honor
  A Millionaire at Midnight
  A Moment of Madness
  A Vengeful Affair
  An Accidental Date with a Billionaire
  Asking for Trouble
  Beauty and the Bachelor
  Besting the Billionaire
  Betraying the Billionaire
  Billionaire Blackmail
  Blackmailing the Bad Girl
  Blame It on the Bet
  Catching the CEO
  Chasing the Runaway Bride
  Coach Maddie and The Marine
  Cowboys Need Not Apply
  Crazy for the Competition
  Dare to Resist

Dirty Games
Falling for her Enemy
Falling for the Bad Girl
Falling for the Enemy
Flirting with the Competition
Gilded Lily
Her Enemy Protector
His Undercover Princess
Impulse Control
Kissing her Crush
Mistress Spy
Once in a Blue Moon
Operation Cinderella
Opposing the Cowboy
Playing at Love
Protecting What's His
Risky Surrender
Running with a Sweet Talker
Spiced
Taming the CEO
Tempting the Corporate Spy
The Dare
The Greek Tycoon's Tarnished Bride
The Kissing Contract
The Last Second Chance: A Small Town Love Story
The Millionaire's Forever
The Playboy's Proposal
Totally, Sweetly, Irrevocably
Your B&B or Mine

Historical

A Lady Never Tells
   A Mistress for Penndrake
   A Pirate's Command
   A Rogue for Emily
   An Artful Seduction
   At the Spy's Pleasure
   Captured Heart
   Claiming the Highlander's Heart
   Distracting the Duke
   Duchess by Day, Mistress by Night
   Enchanting the Earl
   His Pirate Seductress
   His Rebellious Lass
   How to Best a Marquess
   How to Bewitch an Earl
   How to Play the Game of Love
   Once Upon a Masquerade
   Romancing the Rumrunner
   Sweet Home Highlander
   Tangled Hearts
   The Duke Meets his Match
   The Highlander Who Loved Me
   The Scottish Rogue
   Torch in the Forest
   What a Scot Wants
   Wicked in his Arms

Mystery & Suspense

Brazilian Capture
   Hard to Protect

Paranormal

Awakening: Britton
   Bad Mouth
   Beauty and the Werewolf
   Bite My Fire
   Drakon's Knight
   Moonlight
   The Hunt

Romantic Suspense

Armed 'N' Ready
   London Calling
   Prisoner of Love
   Sins of her Father

List of Stories by Secondary Trope

I thought you might find it interesting to know which additional tropes these authors have used, so I've listed the secondary tropes and the stories they were used in.

Accidental Marriage

Wicked in his Arms

Accidental Pregnancy

Duchess by Day, Mistress by Night

Across the Tracks

A Man of Honor
   Beauty and the Werewolf
   Crazy for the Competition
   Duchess by Day, Mistress by Night
   Once Upon a Masquerade
   The Kissing Contract

Arranged Marriage

A Mistress for Penndrake
  What a Scot Wants

Baby on the Doorstep

Falling for her Enemy

Bad Boy/Bachelor/Playboy Reformed

A Man of Honor
  Beauty and the Werewolf
  Risky Surrender

Bad Girl/Rich Boy

Falling for the Bad Girl
  Flirting with the Competition

Bait and Switch

Hard to Protect
  Once Upon a Masquerade
  Taming the CEO

Best Friend's Little Sister

Dare to Resist

Bet/Dare/Wager

69 Million Things I Hate About You
  Blame It on the Bet
  How to Best a Marquess
  Sweet Home Highlander
  What a Scot Wants

Blackmail

A Mistress for Penndrake
  An Artful Seduction
  Beauty and the Bachelor
  Blackmailing the Bad Girl
  Captured Heart
  Hard to Protect
  Mistress Spy
  Sweet Home Highlander

Bodyguard/Protector

A Lady Never Tells
  Armed 'N' Ready
  At the Spy's Pleasure
  Duchess by Day, Mistress by Night
  Falling for the Bad Girl
  Her Enemy Protector
  His Rebellious Lass
  His Undercover Princess
  London Calling
  Mistress Spy

Moonlight
Protecting What's His
The Highlander Who Loved Me
What a Scot Wants

Boss and Employee

69 Million Things I Hate About You
A Millionaire at Midnight
Blackmailing the Bad Girl
Mistress Spy
Tempting the Corporate Spy

Co-workers

Besting the Billionaire
Impulse Control
Kissing her Crush
The Dare

Fake Engagement

A Millionaire at Midnight
Her Enemy Protector
How to Bewitch an Earl

Fake Relationship

Tangled Hearts
The Millionaire's Forever
What a Scot Wants

Fish Out of Water

Cowboys Need Not Apply
  Hard to Protect
  London Calling
  Once Upon a Masquerade
  The Greek Tycoon's Tarnished Bride

Fling

Duchess by Day, Mistress by Night

Forbidden Love/Off Limits

Beauty and the Werewolf
  Betraying the Billionaire
  Catching the CEO
  Duchess by Day, Mistress by Night
  Hard to Protect
  Moonlight
  Once Upon a Masquerade
  Risky Surrender
  The Duke Meets his Match
  The Hunt
  Your B&B or Mine

Forced Marriage

Beauty and the Bachelor

Forced Proximity

Marriage in Trouble

A Pirate's Command

Marriage of Convenience

Betraying the Billionaire
  Tangled Hearts
  The Greek Tycoon's Tarnished Bride

Mistaken Identity

An Accidental Date with a Billionaire
  Betraying the Billionaire
  Bite My Fire
  Romancing the Rumrunner
  Tempting the Corporate Spy

One-Night Stand

A Moment of Madness
  Flirting with the Competition

Opposites Attract

69 Million Things I Hate About You
  An Accidental Date with a Billionaire
  Armed 'N' Ready
  Asking for Trouble
  Betraying the Billionaire
  Billionaire Blackmail

Blackmailing the Bad Girl

Blame It on the Bet

Catching the CEO

Claiming the Highlander's Heart

Cowboys Need Not Apply

Crazy for the Competition

Dirty Games

Drakon's Knight

Enchanting the Earl

Falling for the Bad Girl

Flirting with the Competition

Gilded Lady

His Rebellious Lass

Impulse Control

Kissing her Crush

Mistress Spy

Moonlight

Opposing the Cowboy

Playing at Love

Protecting What's His

Romancing the Rumrunner

The Kissing Contract

The Scottish Rogue

Totally, Sweetly, Irrevocably

What a Scot Wants

Wicked in his Arms

Overcoming Odds

Captured Heart
  Cowboys Need Not Apply
  His Rebellious Lass
  London Calling
  Mistress Spy
  Sins of her Father
  The Highlander Who Loved Me
  The Scottish Rogue
  What a Scot Wants

Political Scandal

The Scottish Rogue

Redemption

Billionaire Blackmail
  Claiming the Highlander's Heart
  Cowboys Need Not Apply
  Duchess by Day, Mistress by Night
  Falling for the Bad Girl

Reunited Lovers

How to Best a Marquess
  Playing at Love
  Sweet Home Highlander

Revenge

69 Million Things I Hate About You
   A Mistress for Penndrake
   A Vengeful Affair
   An Artful Seduction
   Beauty and the Bachelor
   Blackmailing the Bad Girl
   Claiming the Highlander's Heart
   Mistress Spy
   Operation Cinderella
   Sins of her Father
   The Highlander Who Loved Me
   The Millionaire's Forever
   The Scottish Rogue

Royalty

Beauty and the Werewolf
   His Undercover Princess
   Tangled Hearts
   The Hunt

Second Chance

A Pirate's Command
   At the Spy's Pleasure
   Blackmailing the Bad Girl
   Dare to Resist
   Once in a Blue Moon
   Playing at Love

Sweet Home Highlander
The Last Second Chance: A Small Town Love Story
Your B&B or Mine

Ugly Duckling

Prisoner of Love
   The Playboy's Proposal

Unrequited Love

Your B&B or Mine

Tips for Writing Romance Stories

- Make sure your plot scenario is plausible, as is any outcome, while also making your story unique in some way.

- Put your couple into a situation of forced proximity—this is one of the best ways of providing your characters with lots of conflict and tension to deal with.

- Throw a deadline into the story where there is an end point. This will provide both internal and external conflict for your characters, which will amplify the tension and drama.

- Convert a plot scenario from one romance genre into another. For example: take a scenario from a historical setting and write it into a contemporary setting, then tweak the story elements to fit.

- Incorporate additional tropes to add depth to your story and alter the plot.

- Think about the tone of your story. It could be light, or you could delve into something deeply emotional—or even put your characters into a life-threatening, suspenseful situation.

· Have your characters battle with internal conflict that relates to the physical desire they feel for the other person. Incorporate accidental touching or even clandestine touching to raise the heat and tension your characters feel whenever they're in close proximity to each other.

· If your hero and heroine are working together to outsmart an antagonist then they must learn to trust each other, which is another opportunity for internal and external conflict. Individually your characters will have qualities that make them special, so put them in a situation where their only choice is to contribute to resolving a problem using those qualities. This way a discussion, or argument, will arise as each character offers their idea for a solution, but they'll each learn to trust the other.

· Character development is critical. Create personality traits in both your hero and heroine that the other character will struggle to understand.

· Make use of awkward understandings – have your characters be at odds with each other over the importance of things, people or situations. For example: if the heroine has a pet dog but the hero isn't really an animal lover, then have him question her and perhaps get a bit miffed when the heroine wants to take her dog on outings with them. When he gets to know her better he'll discover the reason she loves the dog so much and what it represents to her—perhaps her sister gave the dog to her before she left to get married and the dog makes her feel close to her sister.

· Slow the path to love – draw out the journey to their happy ever after. Gradually build the romance by including lots of romantic/sexual tension, indecision and conflict, and include a range of complications and barriers for them to overcome along the way.

· *What was I thinking?* Put your characters into situations that drive them crazy, making them behave differently, and do things they normally wouldn't. Create uncertainty in their minds at the beginning about whether they've made the right decision. Have them make changes they vowed they would never make. Get them to accommodate the needs of the other protagonist and then second-guess themselves. *What's happening to me? Why am I changing and do I want to?*

· Unrequited love can be a powerful motivator—where one character has romantic feelings for the other, but that person either doesn't reciprocate or is completely oblivious. The admirer may have coped with their existing friendship or business connection, but now for some reason they've decided they no longer can. Yet when their hopes of turning this relationship into one of love doesn't happen the way they'd envisaged, they struggle to cope with the old boundaries.

Final Notes

Thank you for buying this book. I hope you found it helpful with your writing.

The books I write are specifically for romance writers so you can improve your craft skills and become confident in your writing career. I'd love to help you on your way to becoming the next bestselling romance author.

Please visit my website and **sign up** to my mailing list if you'd like to receive my **Romance Writer's Starter Library** – an exclusive collection of 8 handy resources to assist with your writing.

Plus you'll receive an occasional email update when I publish a new book or have useful information related to the romance industry.

If you wish to contact me, please do so. My email address is karen.winter@xtra.co.nz

Good luck with your writing career.

Please consider leaving a review

If you found this book useful I would be grateful if you could spend a few minutes leaving a review (it can be as short as you like) on the book's Amazon page.

Thank you very much.
  Karen

About the Author

Karen Winter is the internationally published author of the popular book series **Romance Writers' Bookshelf – essential craft books for the serious romance author**. Her books are written specifically for romance writers and have helped many achieve their writing dreams.

As a writer herself and an avid reader of romance fiction, Karen has put to good use her background in technical writing and research to create valuable resources that every romance author should have in her toolkit. Her passion is to help writers become skilled in their craft and confident in their writing career.

Karen is a member of Romance Writers of New Zealand and Romance Writers of America.

As you will see from some of the dedications in her books, she is a strong advocate for animal welfare and supports several organisations.

She lives in New Zealand in the beautiful city of Christchurch.

www.karen-winter.com

Romance Writers' Bookshelf

Essential craft books for the serious romance author

Are any missing from your bookshelf?

Available on Amazon: https://amzn.to/2RGMseu

.

Made in the USA
Las Vegas, NV
16 April 2022

47579232R00134